PENGUIN ANANDA

CELEBRATING LIFE

Rishi Nityapragya, a disciple of His Holiness Sri Sri Ravi Shankarji, is the director of programmes at the world's largest NGO, the Art of Living Foundation.

He is a qualified chemical engineer, has had a successful corporate career and was an accomplished motorbike racer as well as a professional singer.

Rishi means a seer, a mentor. This modern rishi can be rightly described as a 'spiritual scientist', bursting with love, energy and a never-dying enthusiasm to serve humanity. With a scientific approach towards life, Rishi Nityapragya has derived many transformative, practical formulas that he calls 'Swadhyay–Self-exploration', which are the essence of his teachings.

His research paper has been published in the international journal *Brain and Behaviour*.

He has been a keynote speaker at various international forums, such as the Parliament of World's Religions, Cape Town; the United Nations Millennium Peace Summit, New York; the Global Dharma Conference, New Jersey; the first-ever Yoga and Meditation Conference, Iran; and the World Health Organization conference for representatives of Southeast Asian countries.

He has conducted programmes at prestigious institutions and organizations, like the London School of Economics, Indian Institute of Technology, Indian Institute of Management, Indian Management Association, Tata Institute of Social Sciences and over seventy universities across the world. He has imparted corporate training at various corporate houses, like Tata Steel, Adani Logistics, L&T, Garware and Kirloskar, and has conducted sessions for members of many chapters of Rotary and Lions clubs.

In his role as the director of programmes at the Art of Living Foundation, Rishi Nityapragya also trains teachers and volunteers, and has taught Art of Living programmes to millions of people in more than sixty countries around the world.

PRAISE FOR *CELEBRATING LIFE*

'In challenging times, this precious knowledge of consciousness can be an empowering guide for young minds to be happy, content and make life a celebration!'—**Suresh Prabhu, member of Parliament and former cabinet minister**

'A human being has infinite potential, with limitless creativity and boundless thinking and imagining capacity. But very often, our inability to liberate ourselves, bound by fear, negativity or ignorance, prevents us from reaching our potential! Rishi Nityapragyaji in his book *Celebrating Life* teaches us how we can strive to reach our potential'—**T.V. Mohandas Pai, chairman, Aarin Capital Partners**

'I am sure this book will provide precious guidance for you to find peace and happiness in your life. This one is a "must have" scripture in everyone's collection'—**Padmashree Pandit Suresh Wadkar**

'Rishiji has given the crux of the whole book in its title itself. His life is nothing but a celebration. When you, the soul, experience your limitlessness, your complete existence becomes full with bliss and celebration'—**Swami Girishanand Saraswati**

'This is actually much more than a book: it is a life guide. Soak yourself in the pure wisdom of the book and feel liberated'—**Karanvir Bohra, actor**

'*Celebrating Life* is one of those books which you will treasure and read again and again. It's a book you will want to digest and live by. It offers such beautiful insight into the nature of the mind. It makes you realize that this life is in your control and that you are in control of your destiny. More importantly, it gives you the tools to allow you to live that. You decide your life. My only suggestion: Get your hands on it . . . and hold on to it until you start living it'—**Anuraag Agarwal, head, strategy, ACG, and board member, Amar Chitra Katha**

Celebrating Life

SIX STEPS TO THE COMPLETE BLOSSOMING
OF YOUR CONSCIOUSNESS

RISHI NITYAPRAGYA

PENGUIN
ANANDA

An imprint of Penguin Random House

PENGUIN ANANDA

USA | Canada | UK | Ireland | Australia
New Zealand | India | South Africa | China

Penguin Ananda is part of the Penguin Random House group of companies
whose addresses can be found at global.penguinrandomhouse.com

Published by Penguin Random House India Pvt. Ltd
7th Floor, Infinity Tower C, DLF Cyber City,
Gurgaon 122 002, Haryana, India

Penguin
Random House
India

First published in Penguin Ananda by Penguin Random House India 2020

Copyright © Rishi Nityapragya 2020

10 9 8 7 6 5 4 3 2 1

The views and opinions expressed in this book are the author's own and the facts
are as reported by him which have been verified to the extent possible, and the
publishers are not in any way liable for the same.

ISBN 9780143450689

Typeset in Arno Pro by Manipal Technologies Limited, Manipal

www.penguin.co.in

Contents

Step Three: Meticulous Refinement of Your Consciousness

The Beginning

I. My Inspiration

I call myself a student of life.

Along with the many different roles that I am playing in this lifetime, the role I most identify with, the most accurate description of how I view myself is, *I am a student of life*.

In this enchanting roller-coaster journey called life, there has been a range of experiences, from pinnacles of celebration to extreme depths of meditation, from heart-wrenching moments of devotion and longing to the most beautiful experiences of dissolving and merging, experiencing oneness with Divinity. Life offered experiences of all flavours, of all shades of colours, and with every passing event, different emotions, varied perspectives and a range of tendencies got triggered in me. The conditioning of my mind into *swadhyay, self-exploration*, helped me immensely in understanding the habits and patterns of my mind, triggered by a plethora of events. The more I understood the intricacies of my mind, the more I was flabbergasted by the power of it. Each voyage of self-exploration inspired me to go deeper and deeper into the technicalities of the consciousness. With every eureka moment, my innate instinct to share my experiences with the world became stronger. Whenever I got an opportunity to share my findings, with utmost sincerity and enthusiasm, I would share them in my discourses, lectures and satsangs. Thousands confided in me that they immensely benefited from these insights. Many among them urged me to document these *Pearls of Wisdom* and a few arranged for small little logistics required for me to withdraw from my hectic schedule, so as to take out time and write . . . Hence this book!

From a very early age, I had a few intense questions in my mind. What is the purpose of life? What are we here for? The conditioning that society, the world is living with seems to be too linear to be true; first, one is supposed to receive education, then get a job or start a business, then marry, have children, and then their education, jobs, marriages and so on. I've always felt that this cannot be the purpose of life. This cannot be why the universe made human beings. The urge to find out why we are here, what it means to be a human being, what is the ultimate goal was very strong in me. In that process of inquiry, at a very early age, I became a reiki master, a Pranic Healing Master, and went through many self-development and self-exploration programmes, like the Landmark Forum, the Core Empowerment Training, etc. Every programme offered a new technique, a different dimension and a unique perspective of looking at life. But the ultimate question of *Who am I?* was still unanswered. I went and stayed with a lot of spiritual masters, asked questions, got a few answers, yet my thirst was not quenched.

In this process of exploration, someone told me about their extraordinary experience of the Art of Living course, the *Sudarshan Kriya*. Curiosity killed the cat! In October 1992, I organized the first Art of Living programme in Vadodara, India, and then participated in it. The exhilarating blast of energy that I experienced during Sudarshan Kriya and the bliss that lingered on, I had never ever experienced anything like that in my life so far. What interested me the most was the simplicity of the Sudarshan Kriya technique, the height of experience and yet the humility with which it was being shared. I wanted to meet the person who had created this transformative programme of the Art of Living.

My first meeting with Gurudev Sri Sri Ravi Shankar Ji was an enchanting experience. In February 1993, I took a group of nine youngsters from Vadodara to Bangalore for the Advanced Meditation Program of Art of Living. After a forty-hour train journey, we reached the Bangalore city office of the Art of Living Foundation—the office is called Gyan Mandir, the Temple of Knowledge.

As I entered, I saw Gurudev for the first time. A saint clad in white cotton clothes, with a beautiful long, black beard and flowing hair, a radiating bright face and extremely compassionate, kind eyes. As I walked in, He was going out. We met at the doorstep. He looked directly into my eyes and, with an extremely friendly smile, put his hand on my shoulder and asked in Hindi, 'Aa gaye tum? (Oh, there you are!)'

I experienced a jolt of energy running through my body, like a small, happy electric shock. Tears of joy welled up in my eyes and an instantaneous sense of recognition with this *enlightened being* dawned, as if I'd known Him forever. As if I had met a long-lost friend. As if I'd come home!

What happened over the next five days at the Advanced Meditation Program of the Art of Living is history. His divine presence changed my life forever. Since that first encounter with Divinity till today, with His guidance and grace, He has opened up life-transforming experiences for me. Very similar to how an unseen presence blossoms a bud into a fully-blown flower, one petal after the other, nurturing, caring, protecting. Throughout my wonderful journey of the exploration of life, having taught the 'Art of Living' to millions around the world, I have had profound experiences that enabled me to filter the Truth from Untruth, *vivek* from *avivek* and Dharma from Adharma.

What I am about to share with you is the crux of two and a half decades of exploration of life—a minuscule portion from the infinity of existence.

I have sincerely followed this methodology: I have written only what I have experienced.

II. Methodology for writing and reading

I want to be sensitive to the range of people who are going to read this book. There could be extremely mature, wise *old souls*, and there could be those who have just stepped into the realm of spirituality. From those who are sincere seekers, looking for the deepest truths of life, to those who are happy, casual surfers. From those who are seeking solace from some traumatic experience, to those who already have the treasure of wisdom, whom I can learn from. I want to be sincere and honest to these unknown, unseen audiences, who have been inquisitive and courageous enough to pick up this book and read it.

1) The purpose of writing this book

From the early age of twenty-seven, with Gurudev's blessings, I got the opportunity to travel around the world. Except for Antarctica, I have travelled across all the continents, teaching yoga, pranayama, Sudarshan Kriya, meditation and the benevolent skills of living life, *Art of Living*. The more I taught, the more I learnt. Throughout this spiritual endeavour of almost two and a half decades, one marvellous revelation became more and more clear to me, that every individual soul is a treasure chest of extraordinary powers. Each human being is bestowed with magnanimous abilities in their consciousness by the creator. And yet, what shocked me the most was that very few people are really aware of their inner abilities. Because of not understanding their inherent strengths and their inability to use them for beautifying their own life, a large number of people end up being slaves of situations and circumstances. In favourable circumstances they are happy, but as soon as something goes wrong, an untoward incident happens, negative emotions build up in them, and they lose control of their minds. Once you recognize your own infinite powers—in Sanskrit language these inner powers are called siddhis—you will realize that nature so graciously has already ingrained all the necessary abilities in an individual's consciousness to create the life that you want and become the master of your circumstances.

My purpose of writing this book is to help you to explore your infinite potential within and celebrate life.

2) A sincere seeker

We play different roles in different areas of our lives. A close look at ourselves gives us the understanding that life has six sections, six fields, six aspects: (1) relationships; (2) profession; (3) hobbies; (4) physical health; (5) social responsibilities; and (6) spiritual growth.

In each of these areas of life, we have different roles to play. In family, with every relationship, your role is different. Who you are with your parents is very different from who you are with your children or with your siblings. In the professional field, your role depends on the post or position you hold. Life is a dynamic, ever-changing phenomenon. From moment to moment, with every event, with every individual, your role keeps changing. To be able to extract the maximum from this dynamic process called life, you need to be ready to change your role according to the need of the moment and what the situation demands. For example, if you are at home with your family and you continue playing the role you are supposed to play in your professional life, it won't work. Similarly, if you carry the role that you are playing in your family to your workplace, it can be disastrous. In the domain of physical fitness, going beyond your comfort zones with a warrior attitude will help you tremendously, whereas in the realm of social responsibilities the attitude of open-heartedness, friendliness and the zeal to help others will ensure harmony and fulfilment.

As we are about to enter the field of spiritual exploration through this book, your role can be that of a sincere seeker, a student. In the role of a student, a non-judgmental, open-hearted, inquisitive attitude is a big qualification. Sometimes your already-acquired knowledge, your beliefs and judgements formed through past experiences do not allow you the freedom to receive and accept a new idea, a different perspective of looking at the same issue of life. As they say, the truth is multidimensional; it is like a diamond with so many facets. From different angles, different standpoints, the same issue, the same truth, looks very different. To be able to appreciate these diverse perspectives and view life from various angles, different vantage points, one needs to be in an open-hearted listening mode, a student mode, a *sincere seeker* mode.

In our ancient scriptures, the learned seers, the rishis, the saints, have given us a formula for being an effective student, a sincere seeker. The formula is *Shravan, Manan, Nidhidhyas.* Shravan means listening, receiving open-heartedly; Manan means pondering over it, contemplating on how it applies to your life; and Nidhidhyas is experiencing the wealth of that knowledge in your life.

In the realm of spiritual growth, whatever you read or receive, pass it through your own contemplation. See how it applies to you, and if you find something that can enhance the quality of your life, that can free you from some negativity or give your life a positive direction, commit yourself to practising it. Very soon your life takes that desirable turn and that precious experience becomes a part of your life. The more you practise something, the more it starts manifesting. Knowing alone is not enough. Many of you already know what is beneficial and what is harmful for you. However, this knowledge or understanding enhances the value of your life only when you put it into practice. Committing yourself to benevolent activities and resolving to not indulge in harmful tendencies are intermediate steps for that knowledge or realization to get established in your life. Nidhidhyas is when that knowledge becomes an integral part of you.

As we go forward, I will remind you every once in a while to be in the student mode. Please grant me the permission.

There is one more honest acknowledgement I want to share with you here. In the field of writing books, journals or articles, there are different genres a writer chooses from. In the *mind-body-soul*, *spiritual* or *self-help* genres, writers generally use these two distinct methodologies. In the first method, fiction and stories are utilized as carriers to convey a spiritual message, with the writer serving an ingredient of light entertainment along with spiritual insight. The second kind of spiritual writing focuses solely on the *tatva gyan*, the elemental knowledge, where the writer aims to describe the deeper and subtler truths of life in a very direct and undiluted form. In my spiritual journey of twenty-seven years, I have been strongly impressed by this type of *intense, concentrated sharing of truth*. This preference vastly reflects in my discourses, knowledge sessions and the personal mentoring I do for thousands of people the world over. Even in this book, I have very honestly delivered only the tatva gyan, the elemental knowledge, the undiluted truths of life and have deliberately refrained from going into too many examples and stories. I have observed that when examples are shared to deliver a point, untrained minds tend to focus only on the examples, missing the actual spiritual insight. As we go forward, you may notice that the purpose of this book is not to merely entertain people through examples and stories. But the seekers of truth, I promise, will find a treasure to ponder upon, to practise, *to make life a celebration*.

During the process of reading this book, you may get inquisitive about certain things. It may happen that it triggers an intense spiritual yearning in you. Keeping that in mind, I have added an important segment at the end of each of the six steps elaborated in this book: *your personal worksheet.* To get the maximum out of this book, I recommend that you take out a little time every once in a while to note down your personal commitments in your worksheet, which will, in turn, help provide a direction to your life.

In short, put on your student cap, get into an open-hearted listening mode and apply the formula '*Shravan, Manan, Nidhidhyas*'. Listening, contemplating, committing to the practice of getting established in the knowledge.

What we are about to begin is a very methodical description of the functions of your consciousness and the wonderful possibilities it offers you to create the life that you want. I recommend, do not be in a hurry to finish this book!

Step One

Play of Universal Consciousness

I. Amazing similarities between modern science and ancient spirituality

At this initial stage in the book, I want to discuss the commonalities that science and spirituality share. As we go deeper into understanding the technicalities of existence, we realize that science has managed to understand matter using instruments and gadgets, whereas spirituality has depended more on meditation and intellectual instincts to understand life. While science focuses more on the laws and principles of the physical universe, spirituality explores the laws of consciousness and teaches us how to deal with them. *As science translates its findings into practical use, to make life more comfortable and convenient, spirituality is about beautifying the human consciousness and making it blossom.* As we go forward, you will see an amalgamation of very scientific technical discoveries almost merging with the guidelines and principles given to us by the ancient spiritual masters, the rishis and saints.

It is extremely interesting to observe that there is not much of a difference between modern science and ancient spirituality. While describing the double slit experiment, which shows that light or electrons can display characteristics of both waves and particles, quantum physicists and nuclear scientists begin to talk in a very spiritual language; whereas the spiritual masters, the seers, the rishis, while describing their observations of the consciousness, the benefits of meditation and the powers of the human mind, indulge in extremely scientific, technical terminology.

In this journey of exploring the deeper realities of life, I came across a stunning discovery: *'As there are laws governing the physical universe, there are specific laws according to which the human consciousness functions.'* For example, the physical universe operates on the laws of gravity, laws of thermodynamics, laws of electromagnetic currents, etc. Similarly, the human mind works on specific principles, rules and technical laws. Its behaviour is not random, haphazard or irrational. Nor is it magical or miraculous. Here's a seemingly contradictory perspective: something appears to be miraculous until you understand the science behind it, and yet one can never acknowledge enough the mystical, mysterious, miraculous, unseen hand of Divinity which is *'Generating, Operating and Destroying, moment by moment'*. For millennia, ancient spiritual masters have recognized and worshipped these three magnanimous qualities of the Brahman, the universe. *'The Generator-G, the Operator-O, the Destroyer-D have been recognized as G, O, D—God, the Almighty.'* The ability to create, generate, manufacture is called *srishti*, the Brahma Shakti. The ability to maintain, sustain and operate what is already created is called *stithi*, the Vishnu Shakti. And the explosive ability to destruct, destroy or transform matter from one state to another is called *laya*, the Mahesh Shakti.

So both in modern science and in ancient spirituality, the methods used may be different from each other, but the *exploration of life* seems to be the common goal. In this book, I have attempted at accommodating both these seemingly diverse perspectives in exploring the truths of life: the scientific, modern, technical perspective, and the time-tested, ancient, spiritual perspective.

II. Macrocosm to microcosm: The interactions between the universal consciousness and the individual consciousness, between existence and you

In this process of understanding existence, I want to begin with the bigger vision, the universe, the macrocosm, and gradually come down to the lives of every individual soul, the microcosm. Recognizing how the collective consciousness, the Brahman functions, we will also explore the intricate functions of the individual consciousness, from macrocosm to microcosm.

We will start with the scientific understanding of this existence, the universe, the Brahman. Using one of the most powerful telescopes in the world, the Hubble Space Telescope, scientists have attempted to gauge the size of the universe. The telescope is placed in an orbit around earth, beyond the atmosphere, so that atmospheric gases do not restrict its vision. Hence it is called Hubble *Space* Telescope. So far, it has seen more than 500 billion galaxies in the universe, beyond which its vision has not yet reached. So we do not know in reality how many galaxies exist or how big the universe actually is. Now if I refer to the spiritual domain, the ancient rishis recognized this limitlessness of existence, and have always called it *Anant Brahman, Endless Universe*. Among these 500 billion galaxies that we have seen so far is our home, the Milky Way galaxy (Mandakini Akash Ganga). In the Milky Way galaxy, there are more than 250 billion stars.

It is a disc-shaped galaxy with spiral arms called tentacles. On the periphery of one of these arms, there is a medium-sized star called the sun, the source of life for all of us.

Around the sun, planets revolve in their own individual orbits. This cluster of planets revolving around the sun is called the Solar System. Like the rings of the planet Saturn, where rocks, debris and gases revolve around its equator, these nine planets are like the nine rings around the equator of the sun. Each planet has its own unique volume and speed of rotation and all the nine planets revolve in the same counterclockwise direction. Now look at the astonishing similarity between science and spirituality. Thousands of years ago, when there were no telescopes, the ancient seers had very accurately gauged the size of the solar system, the positions of the planets, deriving very precise mathematical calculations for understanding the effects of these planets on human lives. These ancient sciences are called astronomy, *khagol shastra*, and astrology, *jyotish shastra*.

Sometime in the sixth century BC, the Greek thinker Pythagoras discovered that the earth is not flat but spherical. Whereas in ancient Indian scriptures, written thousands of years ago, the astrologers and astronomers have always called the earth *bhugol*, or the spherical earth. The third rock from the sun is our Mother Earth, a habitable, friendly planet. Almost 70 per cent of the earth's surface is covered with water, the oceans and seas. The remaining land mass is divided into seven continents, which are further split into smaller pieces of land, called countries or nations. Every country has many states, cities, towns and villages. So, from the point where you are located on earth, from your town, to the state, to your country, to your continent, to the earth, to the solar system, to the Milky Way galaxy, to the infinite expanse of the universe—*all of it* has one amazing commonality. This whole paraphernalia, the universe, the Brahman, limitless existence, is made up of five elements: the earth element, the water element, the air element, the fire element and the space or ether element. To further understand this mysterious creation, when the scientists magnified small portions of different materials of all these elements, under extremely powerful electron microscopes, to their amazement, they found that solids, liquids and gases are all made up of atoms—the basic building block of the whole creation. This minuscule, tiny brick in the building of this creation, the atom, has three components: neutrons, protons and electrons. Neutrons, connected with protons, form the nucleus or the centre of the atom, with electrons revolving around the nucleus in different orbits.

The earth element, *solid*, is the most condensed form of the atom. In this state, atoms are most densely compressed against each other, as in all kinds of solids like rocks, metals, wood, sand, etc. A lesser density of atoms than that is in the water element, the liquids, the fluids. And the least compression of atoms is in the air element, the gases, vapours, fumes, smoke, etc.

In every atom, between the nucleus and the rotating electrons, there is a vast amount of empty space. To understand and explain this better, nuclear scientists came up with a witty example. Imagine the minuscule size of the atom, where the nucleus is even tinier. Now imagine, if you expand the nucleus of any atom to the size of a football, the first orbit of revolving electrons would be almost 1.6 kilometres, or 1 mile, away from the nucleus; that much of empty space is present inside each atom of every particle. So technically, in the earth, water, air and fire elements, which are all made up of atoms, there is an unimaginable amount of empty space, which is the ether element. Inside the atoms, between the nucleus and the rotating electrons, and between atoms, *the whole of existence is extraordinarily empty*. When scientists calculated the amount of emptiness in comparison with the visible mass, once again they were astonished, flabbergasted, almost shocked. The universe is 99.99999999 per cent empty. The visible mass comprising solids, liquids, gases and fire, combined together, is just 0.00000001 per cent. And in this infinite emptiness, some magnetic pull, some invisible force, some unseen presence, is keeping the orbiting electrons connected to the nucleus and not letting them get dispersed inside every single atom in existence.

Look at this breathtaking similarity between macrocosm and microcosm. See how the moon incessantly circles the earth, in spite of the vast space between the two. The nine planets, in spite of being so far away from the sun, continuously revolve around it. And the sun, in spite of being millions of light years away from the centre of the Milky Way galaxy, revolves around this core. Some invisible fabric, some magnetic force, some Divine plan, is keeping the whole existence connected with each other. To understand this invisible connection inside atoms, scientists tapped into the empty space between the nucleus and the orbiting electrons. With sheer amazement, they realized that this seemingly empty space is not empty at all. It is filled with pure energy. In Einstein's famous equation $E = mc^2$, E stands for the energy that every atom, every molecule, every particle, every substance in this universe is filled with. Essentially, everything—from atoms to molecules to solids to liquids to gases, from earth to the solar system to the Milky Way galaxy to the limitless expanse of the universe—*all of it* floats in this invisible field of energy, and these five elements are less condensed or more condensed forms of the same energy.

There is an interesting experiment you can carry out to get a first-hand experience of this amazing phenomenon. Please do this carefully. If you have a powerful magnifying glass, you will be able to see it with much more clarity. If you strike a matchstick and watch it burn through a magnifying glass, you will see an amazing phenomenon. Though the matchstick is burning, the fire never touches the wood—the earth element. You will see liquid coming out of the wood. Interestingly, even the liquid never touches the fire; first the liquid evaporates and then catches fire. If you observe carefully, you will see the earth element (the solid) getting converted into the water element (the liquid), being further converted into the air element (the gases), and eventually into the fire element (the flames)—and all of it merging into the ether element (the space). And this peculiar phenomenon will happen to everything in existence, if it is given enough heat, the fire element. From wood to metal to rocks to liquids to gasses: first the solid melts, then evaporates, then catches fire and merges into the space. In scientific terminology what we call *melting point* is nothing but the temperature at which the solid, the earth element gets converted to liquid, the water element. *Evaporation point* is the temperature at which the liquid gets converted to gases, the air element. And the *burning point* is the temperature at which gases get converted to the fire element. So on application of the fire element the atoms disperse, changing their state from solid to liquid to gas to fire.

In nature, the exact opposite process is also happening simultaneously. Let us take the example of the fire in the belly of Mother Earth. Even after billions of years of creation, the core of the earth is still a red-hot ball of fire. When it penetrates through the thin crust of the surface of the earth, this fire condenses in the form of gases. When the hot gases come in contact with the cool surface air, they become liquid lava, and when this flowing red hot fluid condenses further, it takes the shape of rocks. *In short, both these processes are incessantly happening in nature. On the one hand, on application of heat, the fire element, the atoms disperse, causing transformation from earth to water to air to fire to ether. On the other hand, when the fire element is doused, the atoms condense and transform from fire to gas to liquid to solid. This discovery that the whole existence, the universe, the Brahman is nothing*

but a field of pulsating, throbbing, vibrating energy, and that
the five elements are more condensed or less condensed forms
of the same energy has astonished the scientific community, the
world over. The deeper they go and the more they know, with
amazement and humility they realize that there is so much more
that they don't know. Every door that they open brings them
face-to-face with a hundred more doors that have not been
opened yet.

In the short span of a few decades, what modern science
has discovered is commendable, and yet this intricately
designed existence has left the scientific community
extremely humbled. To understand their explorations better,
nuclear scientists and quantum physicists have always turned
to Eastern spirituality. Seen through the prism of ancient
Indian scriptures, these so-called scientific and technical
discoveries made so much more sense. Thousands of years
ago, when there were no telescopes or microscopes, the
ancient seers, the rishis—I call them *spiritual scientists*—had
discovered the same facts about existence and documented
them. In the pages of the Vedas, Upanishads, Yoga Vasishtha,
Patanjali Yoga Sutras, Bhagavad Gita, Ashtavakra Gita, etc.,
all the secrets of existence are explored and discussed in the
minutest detail. One such spiritual scripture is Yog Vasishtha,
in which, thousands of years ago, Rishi Vasishtha explained
Brahma Gyan (knowledge of existence) describing the very
same truth and naming this energy as Consciousness, *chetna*.
He said that the whole universe is made up of a singular
consciousness and the five elements are just different

manifestations, different forms of the same consciousness. He described them even further saying that the most gross is the earth element and the most subtle is the space element.

In its slow but sure journey of the exploration of matter, science has only reached so far, whereas the representatives of spirituality have gone much further. The seers, the rishis have managed to understand this existence, this Brahman, at extremely intricate, minute, subtle levels. They revealed that this Brahman has three attributes: Sat, Chit and Ananda. Sat is depicted as truth, being. Chit is the consciousness, chetna. Ananda is eternal bliss. The rishis revealed that the whole existence is made up of singular consciousness, and everything in it—from plants to planets to rocks to trees to insects to animals to human beings—all of them are living beings. They are souls, spirits, beings, *jivas*, *atmas*, *jivatmas*. Each soul is existing at its own stage of evolution. There is nothing in this existence that is non-living. Even if something appears to be dead on the surface, if you observe it microscopically, everything is pulsating, throbbing, vibrating with energy, fully alive in there.

The seers compartmentalized these stages of the evolution of souls into different categories and called them 'yonis', such as Sheela Yoni, the stone stage; Vruksh Yoni, the plant kingdom; Kitak Yoni, the insect realm; Pakshi Yoni, the bird stage; Prani Yoni or Pashu Yoni, the animal kingdom; Manushya Yoni, the human or Homo sapiens stage, and so on. So essentially, everything that we see around us, animate or inanimate, moving or non-moving, solid, liquid or gas, from stones to trees to birds to animals to humans to planets, all are individual souls existing at their own unique stage of evolution. And this slow, steady, incessant process of evolution has been going on for billions of years and will continue for millions and millions of years more.

At this juncture, let us take that important step from *the macrocosm to the microcosm*. Let us try and understand how this technicality of consciousness applies to your individual life, to your personal journeys, and how this process of continuous evolution translates into your individual experiences. Let's take an example of your own evolution, which is in the human form now. You would have started by being an amoeba or bacteria somewhere. Maybe in Sheela Yoni, the stone stage, you would have spent thousands of years being a rock, a stone or a sand particle at a very early stage of evolution. You would have gone through millions of lifetimes, would have changed thousands of physical forms, slowly evolving from being an insect to a bird to a mammal to be in the human form now. Even in the human stage, you would have travelled through dozens of lifetimes for your intelligence to be matured enough for you to be interested in *Brahma Gyan, the ultimate knowledge of existence!*

III. Time and space

One more interesting aspect of this existence: the infinite number of souls are experiencing life at their own respective stages of evolution. Passing through different yonis, slowly evolving, learning and progressing, each individual soul experiences this journey of life in two dimensions, two domains:

The space domain: देश (*desh*)
The time domain: काल (*kaal*)

Moment by moment by moment, time is passing and events are taking place, situations are getting created in the space domain.

This topic of time and space has been explored vastly by both modern science and ancient spirituality, and a whole book can be written about the magnificence of the time-space construct. We will address this subject some other time.

In the next step, we will discuss how intricately designed your individual consciousness is.

Worksheet

Make a note of all the 'pearls of wisdom' that you would like to retain from this chapter for your future reference

....
....
....
....
....
....
....
....
....
....
....
....
....
....
....
....
....
....
....
....
....
....
....
....
....

Step Two

Extraordinary Powers, Siddhis, of Your Individual Consciousness

Nature has bestowed limitless powers upon the human consciousness. The more you understand the technicalities, the scientific aspects of your consciousness, the more you realize that you already have all the abilities necessary to create the quality of life that you want. At this juncture of the book, when we are about to step into the realm of exploring our own true nature, let us intensify our focus and get ready for this *inner expedition*.

I. Interactions between the outer world and the inner world

You, the soul, would have travelled for innumerable lifetimes, would have taken millions of physical bodies. When the soul enters the body, we call it birth; when the soul leaves the body, we call it death. Having experienced the phenomena of birth and death literally millions of times, having slowly evolved for billions of years, you have come to this point where you are reading this book *now*. In this *now*, your life is slowly evolving—event by event by event.

In every event of your life, if you observe, there are two sections:

1. Your outer world
2. Your inner world

The outer world is made up of three aspects: people, things and situations.

And the inner world comprises seven sections: (1) body, (2) breath, (3) mind, (4) intellect, (5) memory, (6) ego and (7) the experiencer of life, you, the soul, the spirit, the being, the *jiva*, the *jivatma*.

Let me explain the intricacies of the interactions between the outer world and the inner world. Just as your outer world—the people, the situations, the things—is influencing your inner world, so your inner world is influencing, impacting, affecting your outer world. For example, as you meet different people, go through different situations in life, different experiences and emotions get triggered in you. Some person makes you feel pleasant, happy and positive, whereas some others can trigger tightness, resistance and awkwardness in you. Event by event, the outer world keeps influencing the emotions, flavours and quality of your inner world. Similarly, your inner world also has a huge impact on the people and situations around you. When you are happy, cheerful, enthusiastic, people get influenced by your pleasant and positive vibe, whereas when you are unhappy, disturbed or upset, most people want to stay away from you. They feel awkward and restrained around you. Every individual, according to their own flavour of consciousness, attracts specific behaviour from people around them. Some, because of their piousness and dignity, manage to draw respect and love from the people around them. Whereas some, because of their own negative flavours, seem to repel others. *In the domain of consciousness, like attracts like.*

People with happy, enthusiastic, fun-loving energy seem to attract the same kind of people and situations. Whereas those who have complaining, brooding attitudes seem to drive happy people away from them. Some call it the *'law of attraction'*. Whatever you allow to develop in your inner world, manifests in the form of events in the outer world. The phrase 'happy-go-lucky' is a very real phenomenon. Positive-minded, happy people, create positive, enthusiastic vibrations around them. A brooding, grumpy, complaining mind spreads the same unpleasantness in the outer atmosphere and attracts a corresponding response from people and situations.

The way people relate to you is largely a reflection of your own mind.

One more wonderful fact is that though your life is influenced by your outer world, your individual life, your personal existence is unfolding in your inner world, event by event.

You meet someone and they make you feel pleasant, you meet someone else and they make you feel unpleasant. In some situations, you are happy and in some other situations you are unhappy. But where is this experience of pleasantness or unpleasantness happening? It is happening in your inner world, isn't it? The quality of your life depends on the flavours, the emotions, the thoughts that are generated in your inner world. No matter how good the people are, the situation around you is, if your mind is unhappy and unpleasant, disturbed or upset, frustrated or angry, life seems like a burden for that event, for that moment. Whereas when love, celebration, happiness manifest in your inner world, it doesn't matter where you are or who you are with, life feels so good!

My point is, your individual life is unfolding in your inner world and the quality of your life depends on the flavours or emotions that get triggered in you recurrently. *If you spend more time in a happy, pleasant, positive atmosphere within, you feel that life is good. You feel satisfied and successful. Life is worth living!*

If more time is spent in unpleasant, unhappy and impure flavours in your inner world, life appears to be a burden. A sense of dissatisfaction and discontent creeps in. You might have accumulated a lot of wealth and luxuries in the outer world, but a sense of completeness and success eludes you. Those who do not understand this subtle truth of life seem to be under the illusion that they can measure the quality of life by what they have gathered around them. How fat is their bank balance, how big is their house, how trendy is their car and so on. But what really matters is how you feel within. *In spite of the difficulties and challenges of the outer world, to be able to maintain peace, harmony, positivity and purity in your inner world is the Art of Living.*

II. Functionalities of your individual consciousness

We have explored this before: as there are laws and rules governing the physical world (the laws of gravity and thermodynamics, etc.), there are very technical laws and principles according to which your inner world functions. You will be surprised to know how potent the human mind is, how infinitely powerful the human intelligence is! The creator has already bestowed all the necessary abilities on the individual consciousness for the souls to explore and experience their own divinity.

As you realize how intensely powerful your inner world is, you will recognize that the actual game of life is unfolding *in here,* in the consciousness. Let me explain in detail the functionalities and attributes of each section of our inner world.

1) Body: The temple where the soul resides

This intricately designed physical instrument that nature has created is a miracle in itself. This self-generating, self-healing, self-evolving mechanism has astonished the scholars and practitioners of medical science the world over. Minuscule cells that exist individually form different organs of the body. Sets of a few organs make different systems, viz. the integumentary, skeletal, muscular, nervous, endocrine, cardiovascular, respiratory, excretory, reproductive, digestive and immune systems. Our body structures are arranged into these different systems, each with its own specific function. I am not going into the details of the functionalities of this 'grossest' section of our existence, because a huge amount of research has gone into the anatomical and physiological aspects and hundreds of books are available.

Though this meticulously designed factory keeps running on autopilot, the driver of the car or the captain of the ship is the soul. Desires arising in the mind give directions and commands to this physical complex. Cravings or aversions, likes or dislikes (*raag* or *dwesh*), positive or negative emotions in the mind make the body act in a particular way. After decades of exploration, medical science has realized that many diseases in the body are psychosomatic in nature—they originate from the mind and emotions. Different emotions in the mind create corresponding functions in the body. If the mind is happy and positive, it influences the functionalities of the body even at the cellular level. If the mind is unhappy and negative, it secretes certain toxic chemicals in the body and influences ease or *dis-ease*, comfort or discomfort, health or ill health.

Along with this scientific angle, let us also look at the metaphysical, karmic or spiritual aspect. In the process of evolution, the soul changes innumerable physical bodies. Sometimes with the body and sometimes without the body, the soul keeps on travelling on its own journey. For the amount of time a soul resides in a particular body, by default, it gets attached with the pluses and minuses of that body and its paraphernalia. For example, in a particular lifetime, the package that the soul gets—from the family to the parents to the siblings to the homes to the eating habits to the religion to the nationality to the entire lifestyle—influences the experience of the soul until it leaves that body. This in itself is a very big subject of exploration, which we will take up some other time.

In ancient scriptures, a few learned ones, the rishis, have pronounced that the journey of the soul in the physical body is like an arena of miseries (अनित्यम् असुखम् लोकम्; *anityam asukham lokam*). A few others have called the physical body 'a golden cage' (*sone ka pinjra*), in which the bird, the soul, is entrapped. A rare few have proclaimed that the body is a temple in which the deity, the soul, resides. With sensitive care, maintaining well-being and purity of the body, the soul can use this wonderful opportunity of being in the human form to achieve the full blossoming of the consciousness and to attain Salvation . . . Liberation . . . Moksha!

2) Breath: Incoming breath energizes, outgoing breath relaxes

This mysterious, self-operating mechanism of energy intake that nature has given us incessantly provides vital force, the *prana*, for the functioning of the physical body. As there is a network of arteries and veins to carry blood from the heart to the rest of the body and back, there is a subtle network of *nadis*, the meridians, the energy channels, that carry the energy of the breath from the tip of the nostrils to the rest of the body. It is not only the lungs that take the breath in.

Through these meridians, these nadis, every cell of the body is supplied with the prana required for it to continue its functions and survive. On the one hand, the breath keeps the body alive, and as the breath breaks, the body dies. On the other hand, the breath is also linked to the mind. As different emotions come up in the mind, corresponding rhythms get invoked in the breath. When someone gets angry, the breath becomes faster and shorter. When sadness or depression gets triggered in the mind, the breath comes out like a sigh. When anxiety or fear grips the mind, you will notice that there is a flutter in your breath. When the mind is very happy, relaxed and peaceful, the breath also becomes relaxed and harmonious. Nature, existence, this infinite being of the universe, the way it has created itself, has given us this extraordinarily powerful *release system* in the form of exhalation. *Using your outgoing breath skillfully, you can release or drop any thought, emotion, memory, judgement, likes, dislikes, even any flavours of the ego from your inner world and be free*. It is very much like the delete button, deleting the data from the hard disk of a computer; or like a duster so easily wiping off anything written on the blackboard or whiteboard. While the breath is one of the most important sources of energy for the body, it is also an indicator of the state of mind. It is a release system for the subtle inner world of mind, intelligence, memory and ego. The incoming breath energizes the body, and the outgoing breath brings relief to this body-mind complex. This respiratory system runs on autopilot whether you are awake or asleep; this incessant phenomenon is a bridge that links the manifest and the un-manifest, the gross and the subtle worlds.

Modern science has understood only the physical function of the breath as a means to provide energy to the body. It has no clue whatsoever about the subtle aspects of prana and its connection to the mind. Whereas ancient rishis and yogis, through their intricate explorations, have derived extremely powerful breathing techniques called pranayama (dwelling in the realm of breath). Maharishi Patanjali is a pioneer, an expert, an authority in this field. Through his exploration, he has derived various profoundly effective techniques to explore the deepest secrets of the breath. This transformative scripture is called Patanjali Yoga Sutras. One more ancient scripture that documents the subtle power of prana, the vital force, the *kundalini shakti*, is the Shiv Swarodaya, in which the functionalities of five types of prana and *upaprana* are explained in the minutest details. You may have the reference of Vigyan Bhairav, where Devi Parvati acquires the role of a student, a *shishya*, a *vidyarthi*, a sincere seeker, sits at the lotus feet of her master, her husband, her guru, Lord Shiva, and learns the methodical, technical process of attaining Liberation, Salvation, Moksha . . . attaining the Ultimate, the Infinite. Out of the 112 techniques that Mahadev (Shiva) teaches her in Vigyan Bhairav, many processes are related to the breath.

Modern medical science has understood and acknowledged that many diseases in the human body are psychosomatic. They develop out of emotions. But as modern science does not have any understanding of how to deal with these negative emotions, out of helplessness medical scientists have created a category of diseases called 'incurable diseases', like asthma, diabetes, cancer, hyperthyroid, AIDS, Alzheimer's disease, epilepsy, hepatitis B, multiple sclerosis, Parkinson's disease, arthritis, etc. For centuries, effective use of breath has been known to prevent and cure these so-called incurable diseases for millions of people the world over.

One such miraculous breathing technique is the Sudarshan Kriya, developed by a modern saint, a spiritual healer, a world humanitarian: Gurudev Sri Sri Ravi Shankar Ji.

Gurudev says, '*A violence-free society, disease-free body, stress-free mind, inhibition-free intellect, trauma-free memory, and a sorrow-free soul is the birthright of every individual.*'

A lot can be written about the functionalities and the potential of the breath. At this stage of our exploration of reality, I shall refrain from going deeper.

3) Mind and its three functions

The mind is a gateway, an interface between your outer world and your inner world. It takes the outer world in and it expresses the inner world out.

In the realm of spirituality, while exploring the subtle world of individual consciousness, two schools of thought naturally developed. A section of explorers include mind, intellect, memory and ego—all four modes of your individual consciousness—when they use the word 'mind'. Whenever the expression 'mind' is used, they mean the whole inner world of mind, intelligence, memory and ego. Another school of thought, which has gone even further in its exploration, refers to these four sections as separate from each other. *These spiritual scientists have very intricately identified and defined the three functions of the mind, five functions of intelligence, two layers of memory and a few flavours of the ego—an extremely meticulous, tremendously subtle, extraordinarily minute dissection of the individual consciousness, almost like a nanosurgery.*

As we are about to plunge into the exploration of the functionalities of this subtle inner world, I wish to remind you to put on your student cap. Intensify your focus and get ready to minutely understand the activities of your inner world and how this technical process translates into the experience of your own life.

Let me give the analogy of driving a car here. Though millions around the world know how to drive a car and enjoy the benefits of driving, very few people understand how the accelerator, break, clutch and engine of the car actually function, and a rare few among them know how to even repair these technical instruments of the car. Similarly, though billions of souls around the world are living in this body-mind complex at their own stage of evolution, very few are interested in understanding the functions of these instruments—mind, intellect, memory and ego—that nature has provided us with, where you, the soul, are the driver. Sometimes this meticulous exploration of the subtle functions of your inner world seems to be cumbersome and a bit of a hassle, but as you understand the limitless powers of these inner instruments, utilizing them optimally and creating the life that you want for yourself is not difficult at all. I recommend that we gear up for this courageous expedition.

The abstract, invisible, subtle section of your existence, the mind has the following functions:

(i)   Perception – Observation – Expression
(ii) Thoughts and emotions about past and future
(iii) Offering alternatives and options

(i) Perception – Observation – Expression

Perception through the five senses. Observation of what is happening within you. Expression through words and actions. It is the mind that watches through the eyes, listens through the ears, smells through the nose, tastes through the tongue and touches through the skin. It is not the eyes that watch; it is the mind that watches through the physical instrument of eyes. Look at this interesting phenomenon. Many times, you might be busy thinking about something, but your eyes are gazing at the ceiling or the floor. In that moment, you are not looking where your eyes are pointed. Many times, when someone is talking to you and your mind is busy thinking about something, their words fall on your eardrums, the ears are performing their job perfectly, but you are not able to perceive what the other person is saying. Because the watching, listening and perceiving faculty, the mind, is engaged in some other activity. My point is, through these instruments of the five sensory organs, it is the mind that perceives. This is called *Perception*.

Using the same instrument of the mind, you can *observe* what is happening in your inner world too. What thoughts, what emotions are being generated, what tendencies are getting triggered in you and so on. The instrument to observe the inner world as well, is the mind. This is called *Observation*.

As your mind perceives through the five senses, it also expresses your feelings, desires, likes/dislikes, preferences/non-preferences, rights and wrongs, through your actions and your words. This is called *Expression*.

Perception is out-to-in.

Observation is in-to-in.

Expression is in-to-out.

(ii) Experiencing thoughts and emotions about past and future

Imagine this activity of the mind as that of an ever-ticking pendulum, with one extreme of the pendulum being the past, the other extreme the future and the centre, where the pendulum comes to a halt, being the present moment. The second function of the mind is the oscillation between the past and the future. The mind thinks about what has happened in the past and experiences emotions connected with the events of the past. Sometimes it imagines possible events of the future and experiences different emotions connected with those imagined scenarios. Look how technical this function of the mind, this swing of the pendulum is. The emotions connected with the past are very different from the emotions connected with the future.

For example, anger is an emotion connected only with the past. Can you get angry about the future? No. In the same way, sadness and guilt are always about the past. You can't feel guilty about something that you have not yet done. These three emotions—anger, sorrow and guilt—are connected only with the past; whereas worries and anxieties, fears and insecurities, expectations and hopes are always about the future. While thinking about the future, wishing or planning for something, very often, this imagination creeps in—what if something goes wrong, what if I fail, what if a mistake happens, what if somebody sabotages the plan, what if I don't get the blessing of the Divine, etc.—and a pang of worry or fear develops. As anger, sorrow and guilt are emotions associated only with the past, the hopes or expectations, the anxieties or worries, fears or insecurities, on the basis of imagination, are always connected with the future. The second function of the mind is experiencing thoughts and emotions about the past and the future.

Let us also explore what happens when you stop the swing of the pendulum, bring your mind to be in the present moment and settle down in the centre. There is an interesting experiment that you can carry out. Focus your attention on your breath, as the breath is always in the present moment. Continue taking long, deep, full breaths, in and out. As you breathe in, fill up your lungs fully and as you breathe out, empty out your lungs completely. Keeping your attention solely on your breath, take 12–15 long full breaths. After you finish this process, observe how your mind feels. Notice how relaxed, peaceful, still, almost empty your mind becomes just in a few moments. Notice how effortlessly your awareness of your inner world grows as your mind withdraws from the outer world and focuses on the breath. The thinking process of the mind is like a pendulum, which is continuously oscillating between the past and the future. As the mind focuses on the breath, this swinging pendulum slows down and becomes stable in the centre. As the mind hits the present moment, three experiences dawn. The level of your awareness grows; you experience complete stillness; and minute observations of your inner world reveal that the subtle pleasantness is already always there. If the mind is not trained or oriented to be in the present moment, your experience of life is hampered, thwarted, restricted, because life is happening *Now, Now, Now!*

Look at this paradox: the perceiving, observing, expressing faculty, the mind, is most of the time engaged in the memory of the past or in the imaginings of the future. But when one takes a closer look at life, one realizes that many activities of our life are driven by happiness. Behind almost all the activities of our life, the basic purpose is to be happy. That is when an interesting, very relevant, almost inevitable question arises, *When will you be happy?*

Look at the design of life. It is very similar to a sand clock. In ancient times, when the clock was not invented, they used to measure time using the transparent-glass instrument of the sand clock, where from the upper compartment, through a very narrow slit, fine sand particles would flow down into the lower compartment, one particle after the other. In the design of life, the upper compartment is like the future, the lower compartment is the past and the very narrow slit in between is the present. One moment after the other, the future has to pass through this narrow passage of Now, the present moment, to go into the past. Look at this interesting design of life. Even if you live for a hundred years or more, you will not get to live even two moments together. It is always one moment at a time . . . *Now, Now, Now!* Even when you get angry or frustrated, it is always about what has happened in the past. But when do you get angry? It is always Now. While you feel anxious or fearful, it is always about the future. However, when do you get anxious? It is always Now. Life is always in the present moment. *Now . . . Now . . . Now . . . Now!*

There is a sweet nursery rhyme that teaches us the essence of life:

The time to be happy is now . . .
The place to be happy is here . . .
And the way to be happy is to make someone happy . . .
And have a little heaven right here!

By living in the present, you can give yourself an extremely valuable gift: a precious present, an invaluable *Now*!

In brief, the second function of the mind is experiencing thoughts and emotions about the past and the future, and when it hits the present, it experiences awareness, stillness, pleasantness.

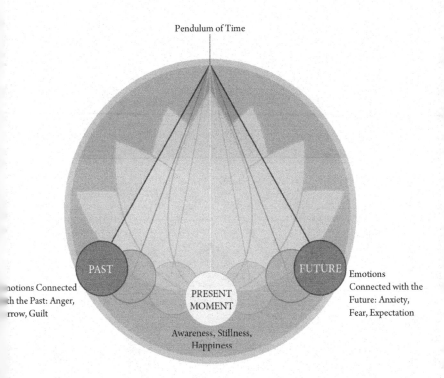

Pendulum of Time

PAST

FUTURE

PRESENT
MOMENT

Emotions Connected
with the Past: Anger,
Sorrow, Guilt

Emotions
Connected with the
Future: Anxiety,
Fear, Expectation

Awareness, Stillness,
Happiness

Life is always in the present moment.

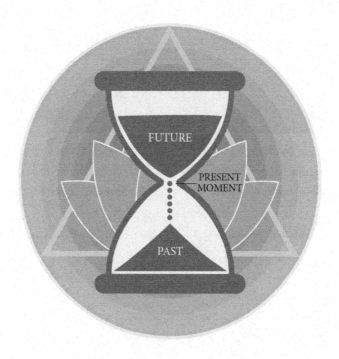

Time to be happy is Now!

(iii) Offering alternatives and options

In this dynamic process of life, a range of opportunities open up in front of us with changing events and situations. In the flow of circumstances, we have to keep responding to the needs of the moment. This third function of the human mind is to offer options for your intellect to choose from in all three sections of your existence: *manasa* (being), *vacha* (speaking) and *karmana* (doing). At the level of thoughts and emotions, we always have a choice: to keep an emotion or drop an emotion. It's the same as having options whether to speak something or not, whether to do something or not. At the being, speaking or doing levels, offering options-alternatives-choices is the third function of the mind.

If we synopsize the functioning of the mind, on the one hand we get amazed at the extraordinary powers that nature has bestowed upon it; and on the other hand we realize how extremely necessary it is for us to culture, to train, to discipline this powerful, volatile, wavering instrument that nature has given to us. In the ancient scriptures, the mind is compared with a monkey, jumping from one subject to another. If oriented in the right direction, it can create a beautiful, fulfilling, celebratory life, but if it takes a dangerous turn, it has the ability to create havoc.

'A cultured and trained mind is your friend, and an uncultured, undisciplined, volatile mind is your enemy.'

4) Intellect and its five functions

Here is a trainer, a teacher, a guide. The intellect is the discriminating, analysing, evaluating faculty. As the mind is involved in its own activities, the intellect is the filter that decides what will stay and what will go, what to hold on to and what to drop, which direction life takes.

The five functions of the intellect are:
(i)   Understanding/assimilating
(ii)   Misunderstanding/wrong understanding
(iii)   Judging/labelling
(iv)   Decision-making
(v)   Logic

Let me explain these in detail.

(i) Understanding/assimilating

As we have discussed in detail, the mind takes in the outer world through the five senses, expresses the inner world out through speech and action, experiences thoughts and emotions about the past and the future, and offers various options in all the three sections of our existence, namely being, speaking, doing. While the mind is busy doing all these intricate activities, it is the intellect that is processing, assimilating, evaluating, fathoming and understanding what the mind is experiencing.

Imagine a speaker delivering a lecture on a particular subject to a large audience. Though everybody in the crowd is listening to the same words, each one's understanding is very different and unique. Many people go through similar situations in life, but their ability to understand and evaluate the situation depends on the refinement of their intellect. Hence everybody's reaction/response is unique. This is because everybody's sharpness of intelligence is very different. There are some people who read something just once and they understand it fully, whereas others may need to read it over and over again to grasp it completely.

As the perceiving faculty of the five senses is the mind, the assimilating faculty is the intellect. Whichever subject you recurrently give your attention to, your intelligence matures in those subjects. That sharpness of intellect gives you a proportionate understanding of that particular subject. For example, some people understand business better because they have given their attention, their mind to it. Likewise, if you look at your understanding of any subject of your life, you will realize this one common technical factor. The sharpness of your intellect gives you proportional understanding of your life. Like understanding somebody's mind, like sensing the possibility of an event even before it happens. What we call intuition or a hunch is nothing but a refined intellect sensing the subtle reality beyond the five senses. If one's intellect has been cultured in the realm of spirituality, one can understand the play of consciousness and human behaviour at a much deeper level than others. If someone has not attended to these subtle realities of life, they don't understand how events happen and what to do about them, and they end up living life dependent on situations and circumstances. Accidentally they feel happy, and accidentally they feel unhappy. Whereas the one who has attended to the intricacies of the human consciousness and has learnt to train the monkey (mind) lives life being a *Master of Situations* and not a *Slave of Circumstances*. The first function of the intellect is understanding, evaluating, assimilating, fathoming.

(ii) Misunderstanding/wrong understanding (*viparyay*)

Sometimes, if you have not addressed a particular subject enough, the same intellect gives you a misunderstanding, wrong understanding or limited understanding. This is called *viparyay*—thinking temporary to be permanent or thinking permanent to be temporary; the truth to be untruth and untruth to be the truth, real to be unreal and unreal to be real. In your life, you may identify how this viparyay colours your perception by making you believe in something that may not be true, may not be completely real. If we observe non-defensively, many of our harmful emotions are on the basis of viparyay, illusion, wrong understanding. Let me give you an interesting example. Receive it open-heartedly. The negative emotions, like fears, anxieties and worries are not based in reality at all. Though they appear to be so real, their basis is in the imagination. You imagine something negative happening in the future, something going wrong, and a pang of fear or worry develops in you. Look at the experience of your life objectively. Out of the thousands of times that you have worried about some issue or the other, how many of your worries or fears have actually come true? With a sigh of relief you will realize that till something happens, till it is in the future, because of the uncertainty you feel worried, anxious or fearful, but as soon as it goes into the past, you realize it was not worth the worry at all. Most of the time, people worry not because the issue on hand is worth worrying about; they worry because of their tendency to worry. In the next topic, we will discuss how these tendencies get formed, how these habits are created and patterns are generated. Worries and fears are not based in reality. They are based in viparyay, wrong or limited knowledge of life.

One more example. At times people do things driven by their tendencies, their *vruttis*, their habits and preferences. You may feel that someone intentionally did something to harm or hurt you, but if you probe into their intent with an open heart, you realize that they were driven by their emotions, their tendencies and their habits. Your own victim consciousness sometimes colours your vision and creates a viparyay, and you see wrong intentions behind people's mistakes. If you pass your perceptions and beliefs through a *reality check*, you may realize that many of your judgements and beliefs about people, about situations, about life, even about yourself, are not complete truths. Sometimes your need to feel good and your resistance to unpleasantness make you deny the *inconvenient truth* and create a viparyay, wrong understanding. Sometimes your tendency to pity yourself and seek sympathy from others makes you put on the glasses of a victim, through which the whole world appears to be vicious and manipulative, which is a viparyay. Sometimes your worries, fears and insecurities colour your perception and create an imaginary bogeyman (Gabbar Singh), which is a viparyay. Sometimes your inferiority complex, your lack of belief in your own strengths, restricts you from living life fully. Even in the spiritual domain, many, many viparyays, misunderstandings, are prevalent. For example, the concept of destiny, the idea that things will happen if they are 'Meant To Happen'.

Later in the book, we will discuss the unrealness, the unworthiness, the futility of these popular concepts. They have become popular because of the sheer convenience connected with them, not because they are real. This viparyay, this wrong or limited understanding, can misguide you from the path of truth, the path of blossoming, the path of exploring your true nature. In short, a sharp intelligence gives you understanding, while an intelligence that hasn't been sharpened enough gives you misunderstanding or wrong understanding. As you deeply understand a particular subject, your ability to understand it even more intricately is enhanced. Similarly, wrong understanding can lead your life away from the truth for as long as the *viparyay* remains. *Truth has the ability to set minds free. It might invoke temporary unpleasantness, but eventually the truth sets you free. Viparyay is the biggest hindrance in the exploration of the truth and is one of the main obstacles on the path to self-realization.*

(iii) Judging/labelling

As we have discussed earlier in the book, everything in existence is multidimensional, like a multifaceted diamond. From different standpoints, different angles, the same diamond appears to be very different. Human intellect has one more function given to it by nature: judging and labelling.

About people, about situations, about any aspect of life, whatever you have experienced, your intellect forms judgements and labels it. You meet someone and if your experience with them is pleasant, your intellect labels them as 'good person'. Sometimes an unpleasant experience is invoked and your intellect brands them as 'bad person, stay away'. And from that point onwards, these prejudices keep influencing your experience with them. Whatever you believe about people, about situations, about life, even about yourself, contributes vastly to your experiences with them. Every individual has so many flavours in them, so many aspects to their personality: some positive, some negative, some benevolent, some harmful, some pleasant, some unpleasant, some beautiful, some ugly. Whichever aspect is exposed in front of you triggers a set of judgements and beliefs in your mind about them, and those labels get reinforced every time they exhibit the same flavour, the same behaviour. That's why the same person appears to be different to different people. Your beliefs, your judgements, your premonitions and prejudices unconsciously seek reaffirmation, and as soon as your intellect sees the same flavour again, it reiterates, '*See,*

I told you so.' In that process it recreates the same experience, and the belief, the judgement, the prejudice solidifies further, in turn contributing vastly to your own experience with that person. If an experience has caused a judgement, it becomes a hook, and similar experiences in the future get hung unconsciously on that hook. In the flow of life, all kinds of experiences come and go. When you are in an unbiased, open-hearted, non-judgemental mode, and when the hook of judgements is not there, the experience does not stick, it doesn't stay in your mind.

Time to readjust your student cap. Look at the experience of your own life through this formula. Your experiences—about people, money or any other important aspect of your life—have managed to form your beliefs and judgements about them, and those judgements in turn create the same experiences again. Isn't it? (अनुभवों से धारणाएँ बनती हैं और धारणाओं से वैसे ही अनुभव फिर बनते हैं।)

Go through a detailed exploration of your own life. In the field of relationships, look at the most important people in your life. What do you believe about them? What are your judgements about each one of them? You will see the same formula in operation here: your experiences have caused the judgements to develop and those judgements are vastly contributing to your experiences with them.

Look at the power of this third function of the human intelligence. If someone has had an unpleasant experience with you and has formed negative judgements or beliefs about you, look how awkward and unnatural it makes you feel. As soon as you are in their presence, their negative judgement influences your behaviour. You feel restrained and claustrophobic. You feel you are not yourself when they are around. On the other hand, if people have had pleasant, happy experiences with you, believe good things about you, in their presence without any effort you feel happy, natural, free flow of energy.

The phrase 'you bring out the best in me' is so correct. Just as you are influenced by people's judgements about you, so your judgements, your beliefs, your labels also influence people around you.

Carry out this transformative experiment: drop your negative judgements about people who are important to you, who matter to you. No matter how real these prejudices may appear to you, let go of unpleasant, restricting, harmful beliefs and judgements, and courageously invoke love, belongingness, friendship, respect and honour for them. If possible, verbally appreciate their goodness, merits, strengths and positives, and see the magic. In a short span of time, the same person might appear very different to you. From different standpoints the same diamond can look very different, and no standpoint is wrong or right, correct or incorrect. It is up to every individual to decide which angle to keep and which angle to drop, which perspective is beneficial, benevolent, worth keeping and which perspective is harmful, restricting, worth dropping. Look at what money means to you, what prestige and respect seem to you. Look at how much your image matters to you, how important spiritual growth is for you. Very objectively, scientifically, non-defensively, look at all the driving forces of your life and what contribution your judgements and beliefs have in each aspect of your life. Even what you believe about yourself is a product of what you have experienced of yourself, isn't it?

The formula is: '*Your experiences create your beliefs and judgements, and your beliefs contribute largely in your having similar experiences again.*'

By now you would have realized how extremely powerful the human intellect is.

(iv) Decision-making

The fourth function of the human intellect is connected with the third function of the mind, which is giving options. The intellect evaluates the pros and cons, the benefits and harms, the pluses and minuses connected with available options and decides which option to choose. The mind gives us options in all the three sections: manasa (being), vacha (speaking) and karmana (doing). From the available options, the intellect decides what to do and what not to do, which option to keep and which to drop. This phenomenon happens on a continuous basis, from moment to moment. The mind offers you the options and the intellect takes decisions. Along with the decision-making process one more peculiar phenomenon happens. As soon as your intellect selects a particular option, all other possibilities instantaneously become redundant, become null and void. Look how powerful your intellect is. As soon as you decide to do something, that decision gives direction to your life in those events, for those moments. Let's take a simple example to understand this phenomenon. When you are getting ready to go somewhere and you open your wardrobe to choose a dress, there are many options available to you. However, as soon as you select a particular dress to wear, all other possibilities become null and void. For that time, for those events, you wear that dress.

Likewise, *in this flow of life, as different events trigger different emotions in you, according to the sharpness of your intellect, you always have a choice as to which emotion to keep and which to drop; which judgement to foster and which belief to release; which perspective to develop and which point of view to let go.* In the section of manasa (being), though it appears to be influenced by people or situations, to let your mind be pleasant or unpleasant is always your choice. In the section of vacha (speaking) or karmana (doing), you can always choose wisely between what to say and what not to say; what will resolve the matter or what will make the situation worse; which option will give you long-term benefits and which option has short-term advantages but can have dangerous consequences later on. The selection, the choice, the decision is always yours. The mind provides options and the intellect takes decisions, and those decisions provide direction to your life. In the Latin language, *cide* means to kill. Homicide equals killing human beings, pesticide equals killing pests or insects. In the same way, *decide* equals killing options. Look at your own life from a bird's-eye view. Look at the important events that shaped your life for you to be where you are today. Look at all the turning points of your life, and look how your decisions have contributed in shaping your life to be where it is today. Look how extraordinarily powerful this fourth function of the intellect is and how valuable it is to select, choose, decide wisely.

If you intricately observe all the options your mind gives you, you will see that every option is a two-sided coin. There are some advantages and some disadvantages. Sometimes small advantages but big disadvantages, or vice versa. Sometimes an initial disadvantage but later advantage, or vice versa. *Vivek (wisdom) is to choose long-term advantages, higher transformation and prepare the mind for short-term initial discipline.*

(v) Logic

Along with these powerful functions of the intellect—understanding, misunderstanding, judging and labelling, and decision-making—there is one more significant function of the human intelligence. It justifies, validates, substantiates *everything* that you do or not do, everything that you want to or don't want to do. This justifying angle is called logic (*tark*). There is an innate tendency of the human ego to always want to prove itself right, to validate its action or inaction. And for that purpose, it utilizes this powerful instrument of the intellect called logic. With logic, you defend or support any activity of your life. There are three types of logic (tark): twisted logic (*kutark*), special logic (*vitark/vishesh tark*) and logic (*tark*).

Many times, we indulge in harmful activities in life, which can damage our individual consciousness. But driven by this tendency to defend ourselves, by using some angle or the other, we justify or validate even these harmful tendencies. For example, people justify their anger, greed, jealousy, lust, etc. No matter how much you defend your anger, every single time you indulge in it, your pleasantness and purity are destroyed. But the intellect oriented in kutark (twisted logic) misses this subtle truth, that the more you justify some harmful tendency, the more likely it is for you to indulge in it. As they say, *'The more you defend your limitations, the more they stay with you.'* This is called kutark, twisted logic.

The ancient seers, the rishis, through their intricate explorations of the consciousness, have figured out all the beneficial and harmful tendencies of the human consciousness. In this book, a whole chapter is dedicated to the subject of the six distortions (shadripu) which dramatically influence your consciousness, resulting in a drastic drop in satisfaction, contentment, purity and self-honour. And it is this fifth function of the intellect, kutark, which unnecessarily, stupidly, almost slimily justifies, defends and validates these harmful tendencies using the twisted logic.

There are some other activities that are very beneficial for enhancing the quality of your life. Many times you need to use your logic to protect these benevolent activities or save your mind from indulging in harmful tendencies. The supporting perspective that ensures the preservation and enhancement of the positive qualities of your life is special logic, vitark. For example, many events have the potential to corrupt your mind and instigate you to do immoral, unethical, harmful activities. To save your mind from these lucrative attractions, you need special logic, vitark.

These proverbs are very good examples of vitark:

God is watching you.

As you sow, so shall you reap. Honesty is the best policy.

Work is worship.

Serving humans is serving the Divine.

These potent one-liners, with their special logic (vitark), have saved millions from indulging in harmful activities and have given very fulfilling, enriching, transformative direction to many a life. Either to save yourself from negative tendencies or to keep your mind focused on benevolent activities, it is the intellect that provides the supporting logic.

Let us take an example of a photo frame hanging on a wall. You need a rivet, a nail or a screw that holds the frame on the wall. Logic is like the rivet and your tendencies are like the photo frame. Your harmful tendencies stay in your mind because of the defence or justification of your kutark. Your benevolent tendencies are supported in your mind because of your vitark. If you do not support your tendencies by your logic, they will naturally fall away. If the nail does not take the weight of the frame, the frame won't stay on the wall. *An inconvenient truth: your twisted logic is more harmful, more dangerous, more hazardous than your harmful tendencies themselves.*

In this event-by-event stream of life, there are interactions between the outer world—consisting of people, situations and things—and the inner world, which is made up of seven sections. So far we have discussed four of the seven sections of your inner world: the body, the breath, the mind and the intellect. The mind has three functions:

1. Perception – Observation – Expression
2. Experiencing thoughts and emotions about past and future
3. Offering alternatives

Connected with the functions of the mind, the intellect carries out these five functions:

1. Understand what the mind perceives and thinks
2. Sometimes misunderstands
3. Judges and labels, vastly influencing your experience
4. Takes decisions from the available options, and based on whatever it decides, creates the direction of your life
5. Supportes all your activities with logic (kutark, tark, vitark)

Whatever you are justifying or supporting is likely to happen again. Look at how extremely potent and powerful your intellect is. Through intricate understanding, correct decision-making and commitment to be happy, pure and positive, as well as by using the support system of special logic, your intellect has the potential to become the guiding force in your exploration of the divinity within.

This is precisely why the ancient seers have given us this guideline, 'If you have to ask something from the Divine, the Almighty, ask for *saddbuddhi* (refined intelligence). If the *buddhi* is *sadd*, if the intelligence is matured, it will keep guiding your life to a complete blossoming.'

5) Memory and its two layers

This is the storehouse, the hard disk of the human computer. What the mind experiences through its three functions and what the intellect assimilates through its five functions get stored in the memory. From years and years of experience, whatever the mind has perceived, observed, expressed, the emotions it has experienced about the past and the future, along with the understanding, misunderstandings, labels, decisions and logic given to it by the intellect—everything leaves its impression on the memory.

This memory has two layers:

(i)   Conscious memory
(ii) Subconscious memory

(i) Conscious memory

This is the peripheral, superficial level that helps you remember who said what and who did what in a particular event. The stronger the event, the more intense the impression, the memory. In the day-to-day flow of life, this superficial layer of memory helps you to remember the events connected with names and forms.

(ii) Subconscious memory

This is a much deeper, much subtler level of memory. In the flow of life, often, intense events trigger strong emotions in you. Many times you must have noticed, as time goes by, the memory of the events fade away, but the intense emotions linger on in this subconscious level. While those dramatic events are happening, almost reactively, you take some decisions and make some judgements. You will see, in a little while, you forget the event that made you take those decisions and form those judgements. However, the blame, the belief, the judgement, the decision stay on in the subconscious memory. This layer of memory vastly influences how you feel, what you believe about people, situations and things.

In this level of memory, one more important activity is happening continuously. Tendencies (*vruttis*) are getting formed, habits are being created, patterns are made. Whatever we do repetitively, creates a pattern, a habit on this subconscious level. These habits form in all the three sections of our inner world: being, speaking, doing.

Being (manasa)

Whatever emotions or flavours develop in your inner world recurrently, their tendencies get formed in the subconscious level of memory. For example, people who recurrently indulge in the emotion of anger tend to develop the habit of anger in their minds. As soon as something goes wrong, something happens against your wish, the already formed, already existing tendency of anger gets triggered in you. Superficially you may feel that you are angry because somebody did something wrong. However, if you look deep enough you will realize that their behaviour just managed to trigger the habit of anger in you, which was already there. If you did not have the tendency to get angry, the same behaviour by the same person would not have made you angry; some other experience would happen. Sometimes you feel worried or anxious, seemingly because of a challenging situation in your life. But the deeper truth is that the situation manages to just trigger, bring forth, the already existing tendency of anxiety and worry in you. For this tendency of anxiety to have formed, unconsciously you would have indulged in the emotion of anxiety repeatedly. If you do not have the tendency (vrutti) to worry, the same situation would have given you a completely different experience.

Different people have different behavioural patterns very unique to themselves. Some people are habitually enthusiastic, happy and positive. Even in the most challenging situations, because of their habit of positivity they are able to save their mind from negativity. Whereas some others have a complaining, brooding and doubting mind; because of their habits, they frequently tend to focus on negativity and make their own lives miserable. The people, situations and things in the outer world manage to trigger the habits of positive emotions as well as of negative emotions, beneficial flavours and harmful flavours, and every time a particular tendency gets triggered, it does two important things. On the one hand, it influences the experience and determines the quality of that moment; and on the other hand, it strengthens the habit of that particular emotion. The pattern solidifies, resulting in the strong possibility of the same emotion getting triggered again and with a higher intensity. It's almost like a person addicted to alcohol or drugs needing higher and higher doses of intoxication. The more they indulge, the stronger their addiction becomes, resulting in the need for higher doses for the same kick, which in turn intensifies the habit further. Look how dangerous this vicious circle is. These positives and negatives in you, these pluses and minuses are your strengths and weaknesses. They form your character, your personality, largely influencing the quality of your life and vastly contributing to the way people experience you and relate with you. A virtuous person—loving, compassionate, friendly and responsible—is generally valued and honoured by the people around, while a person with negative tendencies—like anger, arrogance, jealousy and vengefulness—is largely disliked and dishonoured.

The way people relate to you is vastly the reflection of your own consciousness.

Speaking (vacha)

People who have the tendency to use foul words and slang language, speak the harshest of words at the slightest provocation. The listener may wonder why such harshness is being expressed in such an insignificant event, little knowing that the event has just triggered the already existing habit of abusive speech in them. In the same kind of situation, those who do not have this habit express themselves very differently. Whatever words, expressions, phrases, language you repeatedly use to express yourself lead to the forming of a tendency, a habit in the vacha section.

Doing (karmana)

In the karmana section, too, everybody has their own styles, habits and behavioural patterns, according to how they walk, run, sit, sleep, make hand gestures and so on. You must have noticed that each individual has characteristic body language. The actions your physical body performs recurrently form your habits. Eventually, autopilot takes over and the same behavioural patterns are expressed again and again, consciously or subconsciously.

Thus, the outer world—people, situations and things—is just an instrument to trigger, to bring forth, to expose different tendencies-patterns-habits in all three sections—being-speaking-doing—of our existence. Your personal experience of life, moment by moment, is determined by the habits of your inner world.

If you observe even more intricately, you will see there are two types of habits in all these three sections: *klisht vrutti* (harmful tendencies) and *aklisht vrutti* (harmless tendencies). There are some habits that are very positive, beneficial and life-enhancing, whereas there are others that are harmful, restricting, binding and negative. Your experience of life is vastly influenced by these two types of habits, by klisht vruttis and aklisht vruttis. That's precisely why different people, in spite of having gone through similar circumstances and having faced similar ups and downs, experience life so uniquely.

In this phenomenon called life, whatever we do over and over again, intentionally or unintentionally, willingly or unwillingly, knowingly or unknowingly, creates a pattern.

Sometimes we make it happen and sometimes we let it happen. Sometimes we deliberately do things and sometimes we let things happen on their own. In both these scenarios, whatever is repeatedly done forms a habit. When a similar situation develops, it manages to trigger the already formed habits that contribute vastly to one's experience. On this subtle level of the memory, patterns are carried forward from lifetime to lifetime. The soul travels through cycles of birth and death. When the soul departs the body, the conscious memory connected with names and forms is mostly dropped. Whereas emotions, likes, dislikes, beliefs, judgements, tendencies, habits, patterns, vruttis of the subconscious memory get carried forward to the next lifetime. That is why even newborn babies, who do not have any experiences of this lifetime, have their own unique nature. Some children by nature are happy, energetic and open-hearted, whereas others keep crying and throwing tantrums without any apparent reason. This baggage of klisht and aklisht vruttis is carried across lifetimes in the subconscious memory.

The crux of spirituality is identifying the klisht vruttis, the harmful tendencies, learning to be free from them, identifying the benevolent, life-transforming activities and committing yourself to inculcate them in your life, so that this life can be lived with a higher perception of truth, heightened energy and blissful flavours.

As Maharishi Patanjali proclaimed, 'योगश्चित्तवृत्तिनिरोधः (Yoga is to be free from the tendencies of the *chitt*, the memory).' In this journey of self-exploration to understand the dynamics of the consciousness, we will explore some very powerful, extremely effective ways of overcoming the negative tendencies of the memory. Once you learn how to loosen the grip of these tendencies in your memory, once you learn how to let go, how to delete the patterns, you will no longer be a slave to the chittavruttis. That is when you choose what to keep and what to drop from your inner world, where your personal life is unfolding.

When the conscious and subconscious layers of the memory are penetrated and transcended with laser-sharp awareness, the subtle-most level of the consciousness is accessed. That's when the reality of who you are, the true nature of your unstained, untainted, pure consciousness dawns on you. Hence the seers, the rishis, have given us the practice of 'smaran, simran', repeated remembrance. The learned ones have proclaimed, 'Just the remembrance of this highest state of So-Hum—I am that infinite being—invokes the same experience again.'

A little later in the book we will discuss some magnificently transformative ways to help us dissolve and release the impressions, the prabhavas, in the conscious and subconscious layers of memory, and to come back into swabhava—your true nature.

6. Ego and its types

In the realm of the individual consciousness, this is the most subtle yet the most powerful layer. This ego, this 'I-ness' (main-pan), is your idea, your belief, your impression about yourself, based on your own past experiences. Due to the subtle nature of this ego, very few people are able to identify it in themselves and differentiate it from the soul. Those who have not identified the play of the ego, fall for its games and mistake it for the play of the soul. As you go through the flow of life, in different circumstances, different situations, you subconsciously acquire different roles, you become something in your inner world. As you play a particular role repeatedly, your *'I-ness'* catches that flavour and subconsciously you identify yourself with that flavour of ego. You start becoming that. You start believing in that. For example: I am wise, I am stupid, I am helpful, I am sincere, I am responsible, I am bad, I am beautiful, I am _____. (You can fill in your own blank.)

All these labels, beliefs about yourself, create this 'I-ness'. Through millennia, the ego has always been perceived to be wrong or bad, almost ugly. But there is nothing 'wrong' about it. It is just that the ego dramatically limits your self-expression, restricts your naturalness and creates a false sense of identity. Who you actually are—the soul, the self, the spirit—is extremely powerful, free and limitless, but as this ego, this *'I-ness'*, builds up, you start believing in your limited identity and lose touch with your true, infinite nature. We are about to begin an inner expedition, an adventure that will help us understand these subtle, intricate yet tremendously powerful flavours of the ego and their influence on our individual lives.

Broadly, this ego can be categorized into these flavours:

(i)   Superiority complex
(ii)   Inferiority complex
(iii)   Guilt
(iv)   Victim
(v)   Defensiveness

(vi)   Aloofness
(vii)   Attacking/intimidating tendency
(viii) Complaining tendency
(ix)   Being judgemental
(xi)   Doership
(xii)   Self-orientedness

Let us explore these different flavours of the ego, the *ahamkaar*. Time to readjust your student cap. Time to recommit to shravana-manana-nidhidhyas. Time for defenceless, courageous swadhyay, self-realization. I want to invite you to keep your own life as a reference point to better understand these flavours of the ego and their play in your life.

(i) Superiority complex and (ii) inferiority complex

Among the flavours of the ego, these two are the most prevalent. The superiority-complex ego thrives on people's smallness and lacks, and aspires to be better, bigger, greater than them, whereas the inferiority complex ego survives on the sheer lack of self-confidence, low self-esteem and self-blame. Using various positive or negative points, successes or failures, comparative strengths or weaknesses, you try to be 'one up' on someone or feel inferior to some others. Sometimes due to money, position, age, wisdom, knowledge, physical beauty, etc., we try to be bigger than some people and view them as lesser beings, inferior to us, and experience superiority complex with them. Whereas with some others—

because of the same reasons of position, power, fame, etc.—
we unconsciously feel inferior and regard them as superior to
us. Look at the experience of your own life. You will see that
your sense of oneness, belongingness, love and naturalness
is vastly hampered because of this feeling of superiority/
inferiority. Your spontaneity, your response to the needs of
the moment and your freedom to listen to your instinct takes
a big hit.

Your superiority complex puts on a mask, an image you
are trying to project. There is only a small psychological
advantage, which is a kick to your ego when you look down
on someone. But as you do that, people around you feel
extremely awkward, claustrophobic and unnatural. They
can't be themselves. On the surface they might appear 'goody-
goody', not wanting to challenge your mask of superiority,
but in reality they either want to run away or they tolerate
you because they need something from you. You can't fool
everyone with your masks, your put-ons, your fake-image
projections. Aware, sensitive, intelligent people around you
would have already figured out the games of this superiority-
complex ego.

There is another layer to this reality. Superiority
complex is just a facade, a pretence, a superficial, external
show; underneath it is the actual game of inferiority complex,
smallness, a feeling of lack, a sense that you are not good
enough. As they say, '*Brass needs to shout, Look at me, I am
gold! Gold doesn't need to shout.*' Internally, if you are suffering
from a feeling of inferiority complex, inadequateness, a sense

of smallness, and you feel you don't want people to see this ugly side of you, you tend to exhibit your strengths and virtues to score brownie points, impress someone and be 'one up' on them. A sense of invalidation inside, triggers the need for attention, acceptance, approval and appreciation from people around you.

Often, to get people's appreciation and approval, you either exaggerate or fake your merits, goodness and strengths, but as you do this time and again, it becomes a habit and gets stored in the memory. This strong habit of faking, exaggerating, pretending can become such an integral part of people's lives that they actually start believing in the lies and pretences. That's why every once in a while, a *wake-up, shake-up* reality check is necessary.

Though superiority complex and inferiority complex appear to be the opposites of each other, in both these flavours of the ego the root cause, a feeling of lack, is common. As you learn to identify and release the seed of 'I Am Not Okay', this fake superiority complex—this arrogance and snobbishness—naturally dissolves, leaving you humbled, real, natural and happy.

(iii) Guilt and (iv) victim

These flavours of the ego are intensely destructive and grossly harmful. On the basis of past events, many people have the habit of blaming themselves. Small mistakes they have committed in the past lead them to form strong judgements about themselves, resulting in a sense of guilt, regret and self-blame. The exact opposite of that happens when some people develop the self-pitying tendency of blaming others for their miseries. They believe strongly that people are doing things to deliberately hurt them. This is called the victim consciousness, self-pity, the 'poor-me' attitude. The ego that makes you blame yourself is guilt complex. The ego that makes you blame others is victim complex. Both these flavours of the ego are extremely harmful—they are impediments to the blossoming of your life. Realizing your mistake is good enough; you don't need to keep blaming yourself. Turn that pinch into a sense of commitment and resolve not to indulge in the same mistake again. Guilt is a wasted feeling. In the realm of consciousness, if you want to be free from any harmful habit, from negative tendency, from klisht vrutti, you need inner resilience and a sense of commitment connected with intense *shakti* (power), almost like a space rocket breaking the shackles of gravity by acquiring escape velocity and plunging into outer space. The guilt makes you feel bad about yourself, drains your energy, breaks the strength of your resilience and commitment.

People keep falling into this vicious cycle: they make mistakes, indulge in negative tendencies, feel guilty about them and blame themselves, but in a little while commit the same mistakes again. In order to attain freedom from negative tendencies, what you need is a strong, unwavering commitment, maintained for a substantial amount of time.

Guilt plays a counteracting role in this process. It destroys the strength of your commitment, which is necessary for you to break free of harmful tendencies.

The game of the victim ego is exactly the opposite of this. But before we go there, I want to remind you to be non-defensive and urge you to courageously look at the truth of life. Nature, existence, the universe, the Divine has given us so much. Let us take an example of this lifetime alone. From the time you took birth till today, in the so many years that you have passed in this physical body, look at how many wonderful things have happened to you. How much abundance has been bestowed upon each one of us! From getting the beautiful tool of this physical body, through which we are experiencing this wonderful life, to our family members who trigger so much love and a sense of support and security in us. Look at the variety of colours, flowers, fruits, vegetables, grains and spices nature has given us, for us to enjoy them all. Look at how the sun, the moon, the seasons, the seas, the wind and the rain have played their magnanimous roles in making your life so rich. In the ups and downs of this rollercoaster ride called life, look how the unseen hand of the Divine has always protected us. In the most challenging situations too, through different sources and in the form of different people, help has always come for you. But this extremely dangerous flavour of the ego, the victim consciousness, the sympathy-seeking, self-pitying, poor-me attitude, does not allow you to celebrate, appreciate or even acknowledge all these *gifts of life*. It tends to magnify your losses. When extraordinary benefits come your way, your victim ego never asks, '*Why me?*' But as soon as something goes wrong, this poor-me runt starts cribbing and makes your life miserable.

In comparison with the positives of life, the negatives are minuscule, but the victim ego focuses on the negatives and puts on the glasses of self-pity and blame, through which this beautiful world begins to appear ugly, manipulative, almost demonic. People act according to their own tendencies, preferences, likes and dislikes, but when the victim ego colours your vision, viparyay takes over. Random, unintentional, insignificant gestures by people around appear to you as intentional and manipulative. These two flavours of the ego, guilt and victim complexes, have one thing in common: *they thrive on blaming*. This tendency to blame takes away your ability to respond to what is happening *now*. It does not allow you the freedom to drop the negativities and be free. It takes away your openness to celebrate life. In the process of blaming others, one completely disregards this basic, fundamental principle of life: '*To keep your mind happy, pleasant and positive is your own responsibility.*'

(v) Defensiveness

In this event-to-event phenomenon called life, we are often at the receiving end of scrutiny, blame and criticism. In such extreme events this flavour of the ego, your tendency to defend yourself, gets triggered. This defensiveness takes away your ability to listen and to receive open-heartedly. Many times, people say things inappropriately and express their views with anger, aggression, blame and negative emotions. But behind these extreme expressions, *they are saying something, they are making a point.* If you courageously and broad-mindedly refrain from being defensive and not get influenced by *how* they are expressing themselves, your wisdom catches on to *what they are saying.*

It often happens that you do things that are not understood, accepted or approved by people around you, and they want to bring this to your notice. Many times, people who care for you, who love you, who wish well for you, want to correct you and bring you back on the right path when they see you indulging in harmful tendencies. However, your defensive ego does not allow you to accept their precious inputs. Communication plays a very important role in relationships. When you are able to express your mind openly and people receive your thoughts without being judgemental or defensive, your flow of communication becomes effortless. In such relationships you feel a sense of completeness and satisfaction. You know you are being heard and received. When you have a point to make, you want to say something but the other person is defending themselves all the time and not listening to you, your point is not received, your truth is being discarded, you feel pressured, suffocated and frustrated. These are the exact emotions people feel around you when you are being defensive.

I am not endorsing people's inappropriate, improper expressions of blame and aggression. All I am saying is that even when somebody is in a frustrated, aggressive mode, your non-defensive state of mind can give you immense benefits. You are able to view yourself and situations from different angles, different perspectives and standpoints. Sometimes you might fail to observe yourself, but people around you are constantly observing you. Your non-defensive, open-hearted listening can allow people the freedom to give you precious feedback. These valuable inputs can help you immensely in timely correction of the course of your life. When you defend yourself regularly, nobody around you wants to take the risk of confronting you. They may have a lot to say but would rather not express their views because of your defensiveness. The more they keep these negative points in their minds, the more the negativity ferments in the relationship, resulting in a gap, a rift, distance between people. When you courageously, non-defensively give someone a chance to speak their heart out, and if they say what they have in their mind, the pressure releases, the negative emotions drop and once again an atmosphere of belongingness and togetherness can be kindled. See what happens to you if you have something to say to someone: until you speak it out, it stays with you, and once you verbally express it to them, an emotional load lifts off your chest. Being non-defensive gives you these two immense benefits:

- It gives you an opportunity to view yourself from other people's perspectives, resulting in timely correction of your personality flaws.
- It gives people an opportunity to vent out, to empty out their pressures, resulting in a re-connect between them and you.

It is the function of a mediocre, immature intelligence, driven by a defensive ego that is saying, '*I am not wrong.*' A non-defensive, sharp intellect, oriented in swadhyay, or self-exploration, courageously takes all the inputs and uses them for its betterment and blossoming.

I am recommending a transformative path. Courageously and non-defensively listen to people's opinions, to their criticism and feedback. If what they say applies to your life, use it to fine-tune your inner world and for your personal transformation. If what somebody is saying is a complete misunderstanding, which doesn't apply to your life, listen to them non-defensively for them to depressurize. Let them vent their emotions out. It will relieve them emotionally and you can reconnect with them.

(vi) Aloofness

Of all the flavours of the ego, this one is the most passive. People with this ego of aloofness live life with extreme loneliness and disconnect. They appear uninterested, non-participating, almost cold. Life is a flow of events, and your enthusiasm, belongingness and responsibility give you an opportunity to participate fully in it, as well as to contribute to what is happening, event by event. That's what makes life interesting, fulfilling and worth celebrating. But this aloofness grossly hampers your participation. In this beautiful world of seven-and-a-half billion people, you begin to feel disconnected, unloved and lonely. Your enthusiasm diminishes, your ability to connect and love people gets hampered, your sense of celebration is thwarted.

In the realm of consciousness, each one of us is connected with everyone and everything. The fabric of life is such that all beings support each other. But your ego of aloofness creates a viparyay-misunderstanding of separation. Remember the people with whom you are connected, how you feel a sense of belongingness, love and responsibility with them; and remember those with whom you feel aloof and disconnected. When you are not aloof, you play as a player in this game of life, you participate, respond to the needs of the moment and give your 100 per cent. When this ego of aloofness takes over, from being a player you become a mute, passive spectator and lose the privilege of contributing, participating and making a difference in this game of life. This aloofness is an enemy of the life-transforming flavours of love, responsibility and celebration.

(vii) Attacking/intimidating tendency

As we have discussed, aloofness is one of the most passive flavours of the ego. This one, on the other hand, is the most passionate. People with intimidating ego, with their anger and aggression, put people down. They overpower others with their forceful, vociferous tongue and loud expressions. Everyone around them feels intimidated and suffocated. Usually, the intimidators have a vast reservoir of energy. They can move mountains with their zeal and brute force. That blast of energy, if not channelized in the positive direction, can cause explosions and destruction. Look what happens immediately after you get angry and aggressive with someone. Although you might have a valid point to make, when impatience takes over and you get aggressive, people around you feel intimidated, almost fearful, and they disconnect from you. The sense of togetherness, oneness and belongingness breaks instantaneously. It will take a long time and a lot of effort for that beautiful flow of love and friendliness to get re-established.

In the realm of consciousness, the refined and subtle flavours of love, devotion and compassion are largely destroyed by this aggressive, explosive, sledgehammer, intimidating ego. After you get angry, it inevitably leads you to sadness, loneliness and guilt. Either you want to defend yourself—find excuses to justify your anger—or you feel regretful, guilty and hate yourself. In both the cases your blissfulness drops. Your inner world, your individual consciousness, feels harsh, coarse, rattled. With the fire of anger, your prana is burnt and depleted.

(viii) Complaining tendency

This complaining, brooding, sceptical flavour of the ego is of a passive, dormant, incognito type. It waits for things to go wrong, sceptically observes what is not okay, and whenever it gets an opportunity it unanticipatedly carries out a camouflaged, stealthy assault that takes the form of complaints. In the flow of life, everything, either of the outer world or of the inner world, is a two-sided coin. Everything has advantages and disadvantages, positives and negatives, strengths and weaknesses. A wise, free, Dharma-oriented mind looks for the positives and celebrates them; identifies the negatives and drops them; ponders over problems to find solutions and moves on; maintains harmony and goodness in the inner world as well as in the outer world.

The game of the complaining ego is to focus on the negatives—on mistakes and faults—and to complain about them; to pull someone down to be one up; to prove someone *wrong* to be *right*. You will notice a peculiar behaviour of these complainers. When they go into the complaining mode, and if you try explaining things to them or offering solutions to the issues they are complaining about, they want neither the solutions nor the explanations. Because in those moments, the complaining ego wants to be right, at the cost of someone else being wrong. But look at what it does to the people around. Nobody wants to be with a cribbing, complaining, whining person. Most people feel that complainers drain their energy and sap their enthusiasm. So inevitably, the complainers find themselves deserted and alone. Look at the dynamics of life. In this event-by-event flow, when things go wrong, you have these two options to choose from:

- To take responsibility, find solutions and respond to the needs of the moment even in those adverse situations.
- To crib and complain about what has gone wrong and who was at fault; to blame people and make the whole atmosphere vicious and negative.

The complaining ego thrives on the small psychological advantage of *being right at the cost of making someone else wrong*. In the larger scheme of things, the complainers are the losers, as every complaint hooks you to the past, whereas life is happening *Now*.

(ix) Being judgemental

This flavour of the ego, 'being judgemental', appears very similar to superiority complex. However, I feel it has its own distinct flavour. Hence it is necessary that you understand this subtle yet powerful flavour of the ego and its influence specifically on your relationships. As we have discussed earlier, every individual is like a diamond with multiple facets—some positives, some negatives, some strengths, some weaknesses—and during different events, different facets come to the forefront, get exposed, get triggered.

(Please refer to the judging and labelling function of the intellect.)

A gentle reminder to put on your student cap and embark on courageous swadhyay, self-analysis. Look at your relationships. Using the function of the intellect of judging and labelling, look how the ego of being judgemental plays the game of right and wrong. Remember the relationships where you are being judgemental. Look at how people's negative tendencies, weaknesses, shortcomings or mistakes of the past have stayed on with you even today in the form of your judgements and blames. Look how this judgementalism hampers your free flow of energy with them; look how your open-hearted communication is thwarted; look how your judgements have prevented you from appreciating and celebrating their goodness and positives. Look how difficult it is for your ego to drop these judgements and accept the people and situations as they are. In this ever-flowing incessant river of life, judgements are like big boulders causing unnecessary resistance and turbulence. *Courageously drop the judgements, be free, invoke love and celebrate life.*

(x) Doership

Let us understand this dangerously influential ego of doership. Largely a product of the accomplishments and successes of your past, this ego is a shadow of doership. Very similar to how mistakes of the past leave you feeling guilty and regretful, the ego of doership stems from strengths, positives and achievements. Life is a dynamic process of changing events, situations and circumstances. When something good happens through you, you achieve something, success comes your way, it often leaves the impression of 'doership' on your mind, giving rise to the idea that *'I am great'*, *'I did something great'*. I am not saying it is wrong to feel this way. But if this shadow of doership stays with you, look how it influences your behavior with the people around you. You expect people to appreciate you, acknowledge your accolades, and subtly and unconsciously you start feeling superior to them. This load of doership vastly hooks you to the self-glory of the past, leaving you less natural, less real, heavy and restrained. In the Hindi language there is a beautiful proverb: नेकी कर और दरिया में डाल (Do good, be good and throw the doership into the ocean).

(xi) Self-orientedness

Last but not the least, this one is among the most subtle flavours of the ego. It is like a silent, invisible, platform under many activities of your life. If you observe the thought process behind whatever you do from morning to night, day after day, you will see that almost compulsively, this subtle flavour of self-orientedness is present in almost all your activities. *What about me? What will I get? What is in it for me? Why should I do this?* These questions are the driving force of many of your actions and decisions. This subtle 'I-Me-Mine' is perpetually at the driving seat. On the one hand, it appears to be a self-protecting, self-defending mechanism. In today's time, it is almost like a virtue. 'Take care of yourself', 'fend for yourself', 'you are on your own' are the driving concepts, with people at large becoming more and more self-centred, selfish, almost alone in this beautiful world of billions of people. On the other hand, this 'I-Me-Mine' very subtly disconnects you from people, takes away your openness to include and accommodate the people around you, almost kills your compassion and sense of responsibility that offers a beautiful opportunity to be useful to someone in need. Once again, I am really not saying it is wrong to have this ego. *All I am saying is, every moment is an opportunity for connecting with your fellow beings, taking up higher responsibilities and participating fully in this flow of life. Self-orientedness, selfishness and self-centredness restrict your arena of playing, your area of influence and your overall game of life.*

There is another aspect of the ego that takes us almost in the opposite direction. If, on the one hand, because of its dangerous influence on the quality of your life, the ego is vastly considered to be negative, it can, on the other hand, become an extraordinary driving force, a source of motivation for a lot of people. We see many cases where extreme determination stemming from this I-ness has created miracles. It has motivated people to achieve heroic stuff with courage, commitment and resilience. In ancient scriptures, this I-ness, this ego has been segregated into three categories: *tamasik*, *rajasik* and *satvik*. As the learned ones have proclaimed, the tamasik ego, is delusional and misguiding; the rajasik ego is driven by the zeal to achieve something, to prove yourself and make your mark in the world; whereas the satvik ego is the I-ness of goodness, of Dharma, of righteousness. In the process of achieving complete freedom, the final frontier is to dissolve even this satvik ego and become one with the Divine.

Recap

At this juncture in the book, having covered a range of topics in the exploration of life, I feel it is time for a small recap. When we read or hear something for the first time, the intellect is still in the process of assimilating the subject. When the same topics are recapped, the understanding solidifies further. Let us take this opportunity to consolidate this exploration of the consciousness for the benefit of our own lives.

Existence, the universe, is made up of a singular consciousness, manifesting in the form of five elements—earth, water, air, fire and ether. The universal consciousness, the *paramatma,* has three basic attributes, swabhava, the basic nature of Sat-Chit-Ananda. The journey of each soul, 'individual consciousness', consists of two dimensions: space and time, desh and kaal. From this macro scale of understanding the limitless, infinite Brahman, when we bring our focus to the journeys of individual souls, life appears as an event-to-event phenomenon. Each soul would have passed through many stages of evolution, the yonis, experiencing, learning, evolving, passing through thousands and thousands of lifetimes to be here today, and this eternal journey will continue forever. I call it *Anant Yatra*.

In the journey of each individual soul, in each event, life has two sections: outer world and inner world. The outer world is made up of people, things and situations (*vyakti-vastu-paristhiti*).

And the inner world consists of seven sections:

1. Body
2. Breath
3. Mind
4. Intellect
5. Memory
6. Ego
7. Soul

For each individual soul, the outer world is just an excuse or a trigger that invokes different flavours in the inner world. The actual game of life is unfolding in the inner world of mind, intelligence, memory and ego for each one of us. Pleasant, happy, positive flavours beautify life and expand the consciousness, resulting in a sense of exhilaration, fulfilment and celebration. Unpleasant, unhappy, negative flavours make life cumbersome, ugly, almost a burden. Whichever flavour regularly develops in your inner world forms patterns, habits, vruttis. Unpleasant flavours form harmful tendencies, klisht vruttis. Pleasant flavours form beneficial tendencies, aklisht vruttis.

'Sometimes we make it happen, sometimes we let it happen.'
Sometimes you deliberately invoke a particular flavour and sometimes you let the flavour develop in you. In both these instances, repeated indulgence causes the formation of tendencies. Situations or people's behaviour trigger these already formed tendencies, reinforcing the same flavours influencing the quality of your life.

Play of your inner world

1) Body

It is the physical factory carrying out instructions and orders from the subtle layers of mind, intellect, memory and ego. The eleven systems of the body work on autopilot, keeping this extremely intricate industry running.

2) Breath

On the 'gross' level, the incoming breath provides the energy, the prana, for the body to function. On the subtle level, the outgoing breath provides a release system, a delete button for the inner world to drop anything and be free.

3) Mind and its three functions

(i)   Perception – Observation – Expression
        Perception: Taking the outer world in through the five
        senses of watching, listening, smelling, tasting, touching.

Observation: Being a witness, an observer to what is happening in your inner world.

Expression: Using speech and action (vacha and karmana) to express the inner world out.

(ii)   Thoughts and emotions about past and future

Anger, sorrow and guilt are connected with the past; anxiety, fear and expectations are connected with the future; awareness, stillness and pleasantness are in the present moment.

(iii) Giving options, providing choices at the manasa-vacha-karmana (being-speaking-doing) sections.

4) Intellect and its five functions

(i)   Understanding, assimilating, evaluating: In any field of life, your level of understanding and wisdom depends on the sharpness of your intelligence. The more you understand, the clearer your vision, the wiser your decisions and the better the quality of your life.

(ii)   Viparyay: Misunderstanding, limited or wrong understanding. Hallucinating, perceiving what's true to be untrue and what's untrue to be true. Thinking of the temporary as the permanent and of the permanent as the temporary. Less sharpened, blunt intelligence is a dangerously misguiding tool. It is like having a faulty compass in the middle of a turbulent ocean or a defective GPS (Global Positioning System) in a strange country. A constant 'reality check' is necessary to bring your life back on the path of truth.

(iii) Judging and labelling: The whole existence is a multifaceted diamond. As soon as you form a judgement or attach a label to anybody or anything, you fix your awareness on a particular facet of their existence from the range of available perspectives and make that your reality. Your experiences form your judgements/beliefs, and your judgements/beliefs cause the same experiences to manifest again. अनुभवों से धारणाएँ बनती हैं और धारणाओं से वैसे ही अनुभव फिर बनते हैं।

(iv) Decision-making: The intellect chooses from the options and alternatives that the mind provides. Some options offer short-term benefits, temporary pleasure and a false sense of freedom. Other options give you long-term benefits and long-lasting joy but demand initial discipline and commitment. An unsharpened, mediocre intellect seeks instant gratification, short-term benefits but suffers the consequences for a long time. A highly evolved, mature intellect doesn't mind temporary efforts and disciplines, but chooses long-term transformative benefits. Whatever you decide to do gives direction to your life and all the other options instantaneously fall away and become redundant. Use this extraordinarily powerful tool of intellect in choosing the life that you want to live. Design your life with wisdom and courage.

(v) Logic: This validating, justifying support structure supports everything—stupidly supports the harmful tendencies by kutarka (twisted logic)—wisely protects benevolent activities by providing vitarka (special logic), and habitually, almost unnecessarily and unawaredly keeps providing tark (supporting logic) to insignificant, day-to-day activities too.

In the realm of consciousness, one formula remains constant: *'The more you justify something, the more it stays with you.'*

With these five magnificently powerful functions, this infinitely potent intellect can *make or break your life*. Hence, the ancient rishis have proclaimed, *'An unsharpened, immature, blunt intelligence is your enemy and a wise, cultured and mature intelligence is your biggest friend.'*

5) Memory

This storehouse, this hard disk is designed to gather-download-retain and also to let go-release-delete. All the experiences of the mind, the five functions of the intellect and flavours of the ego with their frequency and intensity, get stored in the hard disk of this human super computer, in either the conscious or the subconscious memory. Vruttis and patterns are formed in the manasa-vacha-karmana sections. Some klisht (harmful) tendencies as well as some aklisht (harmless) tendencies are carried forward to subsequent lifetimes. Your experience of life vastly depends on these tendencies. In the process of spiritual evolution, a lot of emphasis is given to being free from chittavruttis, the habits ingrained in the deeper layers of memory. The freer your mind gets from these patterns and habits, the wiser is your response to the needs of the moment, resulting in better decision-making on your part that spontaneously culminates into a benevolent, celebratory life. As these impressions, emotions, beliefs, judgements, klisht and aklisht vruttis are regularly released—effortlessly, spontaneously, almost naturally—the soul retains the remembrance of its true nature of pure untainted consciousness.

6) Ego

This is the most subtle layer of your inner world and its different flavours are the most powerful driving forces of your life. Look how many people are indulging in what all activities driven by the different flavours of the ego. Open-heartedly and courageously look at the effect these flavours have on your individual life and on the lives of those around you.

(i)   Superiority complex: Just a facade, wanting to hide the smallness, portraying and exhibiting your strengths and positives, trying to impress people and score brownie points, while underneath it all, an inferiority complex lurks.

(ii)   Inferiority complex: The root cause behind many negative emotions like fear, insecurity, jealousy, etc.

(iii)   Guilt complex: A wasteful feeling. It breaks your courage, commitment and resilience required for you to give up your negative tendencies.

(iv)   Victim complex: Your biggest enemy. Plunges you deep into the darkness of viparyay (wrong knowledge); makes you a self-pitying and sympathy-seeking person; prevents you from taking responsibility for your own life, thereby causing great damage.

(v)   Defensiveness: When this defensive ego is at the driving seat, it completely destroys sincere seeking, swadhyay (self-exploration). It defends itself almost compulsively, justifies the wrongs, denies the most blatant truths, hides like a coward and dishonestly pretends and fakes. In the process of being free from negative habits, the first necessity is to open-heartedly acknowledge your harmful tendencies and commit yourself to be free from them. The defensive ego misses this vital step and the vicious cycle continues: First, people indulge in harmful tendencies, compulsively defend and justify themselves. The more they justify, the more they indulge in the same habits repeatedly. This in turn results in the calcification of these harmful tendencies.

(vi)   Aloofness: This passive, dormant, unassertive flavour of the ego causes extreme loneliness, disconnection, almost depression. It takes away your will to participate in anything, your sense of responsibility and enthusiasm, and your desire to celebrate life.

(vii) Attacking/intimidating tendency: This intimidating, aggressive, attacking flavour of the ego destroys the subtle, soft, refined flavours of love, compassion, devotion and beauty.

(viii) Complaining tendency: This brooding, cribbing, complaining flavour of the ego focuses on insignificant negativities and magnifies them. It needs to prove people 'wrong' for it to be 'right'. In order to solve problems and issues of life, one needs resilience, positivity and a sense of responsibility. The complaining ego kills all these virtues and gets you hooked to the past.

(ix) Being judgemental: Your judgements, grudges and prejudices fix your awareness to a particular facet of the diamond, vastly influencing your future experiences. Your experiences form your judgements and beliefs, and your judgements cause the same experiences to happen again.

(x) Doership: Your successes, your accomplishments, your achievements form this shadow of doership. When this doership ego solidifies, it makes you lose your naturalness, realness and humility. It creates the false sense that you are better than others.

(xi) Self-orientedness: This self-inflicted 'I-Me-Mine' takes away the friendly, loving togetherness, vastly restricting your usefulness, responsibility and generosity.

These eleven flavours of the ego share one commonality: recurrent indulgence in these flavours leads to the formation of habits, which inevitably result in separation, disconnection, loneliness. They dramatically reduce love, belongingness and oneness with people. *In life, love brings the biggest security, and to lose love is the biggest fear in the world.* When this beautiful flavour of belongingness, friendliness, love gets thwarted because of these flavours of the ego, fear and insecurity grip your mind. When, because of the ego, love disperses, fear takes over. Insecurity intensifies.

At this juncture, having recapped all the topics that we have covered so far, you must try to identify the flavours of the ego that come up in you and observe how they influence your relationships and your overall experience of life. You will notice an amusing phenomenon: as soon as you identify the flavours of your ego, the process of achieving freedom from it instantaneously begins. Hence the learned ones, the rishis, have proclaimed, *'The ego can survive only in the darkness of ignorance.'*

7) Self – Soul – Jiva – Jivatma

This infinitely powerful sphere of consciousness is the 'experiencer' of life. In this ocean of consciousness, the universe, the Brahman, the *paramatma* , this is the wave, the soul, the jivatma. Made from the same water, on one level the wave has its own individual existence separate from other waves, yet from a broader perspective, from a bird's-eye view, the wave is the ocean. Isn't it? Similarly, at the micro level, every individual soul has its unique personal existence, separate from the other souls. But from a cosmic standpoint, the soul is the Brahman, the universe. The rishis, the enlightened beings, having explored this ultimate truth, have described this magnificent experience in their own unique ways. According to the four Vedas, the four *mahavakyas* indicate the ultimate unity of the individual consciousness-jivatma with supreme consciousness-paramatma.

These four mahavakyas are:

- *Pragnanam Brahma* – प्रज्ञानम् ब्रह्म
  '*It is a knowing universe.*' Comes from an Upanishad related to the Rig Veda.

- *Aham Brahma Asmi* – अहम् ब्रह्मास्मि
  '*I am the Brahman*'; '*I am the Universe*'; '*the Self is Brahman*'. It is from an Upanishad related to the Yajur Veda.

- *Tat Tvam Asi* – तत्वमसि
  '*You are That.*' It is from the Chandogya Upanishad related to the Sama Veda.

- *Ayam Atma Brahma* – अयं आत्मा ब्रह्म
  '*The atma, the soul, the self is Brahman.*' It reveals the nonduality between atma and Brahman, between the soul and the universe. It comes from the Mandukya Upanishad related to the Atharva Veda.

Travelling through millions of lifetimes, passing through numerous yonis, using the instruments of body, breath, mind, intelligence, memory and ego, the soul experiences life, learns and evolves, and ultimately attains Salvation, Liberation, Nirvana, Moksha, merging back into the ocean, the paramatma. For centuries, inquisitive students and spiritual seekers have tried to understand why the soul separates from the Brahman in the first place, passes through millions of lifetimes of separation and it ultimately becomes wise enough to merge back into Divine existence. To explore the reason and the purpose of this separation many have formed their own theories, while a few others, out of frustration, have even given up the quest. A rare few enlightened beings, the rishis, the spiritual masters, have revealed that this experience of separation of the soul and the Brahman is nothing but an illusion created by the play of Maya, and the whole spiritual journey is for the soul to realize this illusion. The rishis, with optimum devotion and reverence towards the Divine, have proclaimed that the ultimate truth of existence is that the universe, the paramatma, the Brahman is one singular living being and 'everything' in it is part of that singular Divinity.

To be able to sit at the lotus feet of an enlightened master, my Gurudev, to be able to experience this ultimate truth and to be able to express it in its purest form . . . What a blessing! What a blessing! What a blessing!

SOUL
EGO
MEMORY
INTELLECT
MIND
— BREATH

BODY

Seven layers of your inner world

Worksheet

Make a note of all the 'pearls of wisdom' that you would like to retain from this chapter for your future reference

....
....
....
....
....
....
....
....
....
....
....
....
....
....
....
....
....
....
....
....
....
....
....
....

Make a list of the flavours of the ego that come up in you regularly and note down their effects in all areas of your life

....

....

....

....

....

....

....

....

....

....

....

....

....

....

....

....

....

....

....

....

....

....

....

....

....

Step Three

Meticulous Refinement of Your Own Consciousness

I. Understanding the process of evolution

As we understand the play of consciousness more and more, the process of evolution of an individual soul becomes clear. The evolution of an individual soul is nothing but the expansion, maturity and refinement of the individual consciousness. Any soul in its own journey, passing through millions of lifetimes, graduating to higher and higher yonis, is exploring, learning and knowing subtler and deeper truths of life. It is pulsating, resonating and vibrating at higher and higher frequency of energy and is experiencing intensified levels of the different flavours of bliss, like love, compassion, celebration, valour, dispassion, etc. In short, the evolution of an individual soul is nothing but incessant expansion, refinement and intensifying of the individual consciousness.

One more intricate observation. In your own life, look at all the activities that you do from morning to night, day after day—from studying to working to managing homes and families to watching movies to meditating. What is the purpose behind all these activities, behind anything and everything that you do? Why do you do whatever you do? If you observe minutely and sensitively, you will see that some of your activities are driven by the knowledge or information you have already acquired. You have understood and assimilated the value of a particular activity, the importance of it, the benefit it can bring to your life, and that understanding drives you to participate in those activities on a regular basis. At other times, your desire to know something and your curiosity to explore deeper and higher truths become the driving force for a few selective activities of your life. In short, your desire to know and what you know so far are at the driving seat, and the truth is the driving force. There are some other activities you want to carry out in order to enhance your energy levels. For example, if you feel tired, you want to sleep; if you feel hungry and drained out of energy, you want to eat. Many practise pranayama to heighten their energy levels.

In other words, some activities of your life are driven by what you already know or what you want to know, while some other activities are driven by your heightened energy levels or by your desire to enhance your energy levels. But close observation will reveal that the driving force behind most activities in the whole of existence is Ananda, the different flavours of bliss. Happiness, pleasure, *sukh* is the purpose. Ask this basic question to anybody in the world: *'Why are you doing whatever you are doing?'* The most honest, most sincere and most frequent answer would be: *'We want to be happy and want to avoid unhappiness.'* For centuries, these different flavours of Ananda have inspired the whole existence and everybody in it to do extraordinary things. Look at what love does to you. Look how patriotism, valour, love for the nation drive people to do heroic stuff. Look how the mild, humbling flavour of compassion compels you to serve and reach out to those in need. Look how the flavours of enthusiasm and celebration have been the driving force for millions around the globe. Look how the naughty, mischievous, cheeky flavours in people have created fun and laughter. Look how centred, dispassionate, dignified stillness in someone causes your heart to bow down with reverence. *At their own stages of evolution, every single soul is expressing all these flavours of Ananda in their own unique way—from gushing winds to flowing rivers to chirping birds to playing animals to celebrating or meditating humans. The whole existence is a play of Ananda-bliss.*

Look at this astonishingly beautiful design of existence. Sat-Chit-Ananda are the basic attributes, the swabhava, of the consciousness, of Brahman. The progress, the evolution of the individual soul is nothing but a process of slow, steady, incessant refinement, maturity and blossoming of the individual consciousness. All the activities that the soul carries out in its individual journey are purely driven by the play of consciousness. What I mean is, something that is your very nature is also the driving force of your life. The enhancement, intensification, refinement and maturity of your basic nature is what the whole process of evolution is, and the experience of your own life would vastly depend on the stage of your own evolution.

One more breathtaking truth: '*The nature of nature is to evolve.*' Look around you, very slowly, steadily, incessantly, almost unstoppably the whole existence, and every particle in it, is constantly evolving by itself. Every individual soul is refining their individual consciousness. Sometimes life grows in the most hostile, non-supporting, adverse situations. Sometimes in a concrete wall you see a plant finding its own root; sometimes you see infants who lost both their parents at the time of birth, and yet life finds its own ways to persist. For billions and billions of years, this incessant, slow and steady process of evolution has continued.

Let me give you an example of driving an automatic car. If you start an automatic car, put it in drive gear and remove your foot from the brake paddle, even if you do not apply the accelerator, at a very slow pace, the car will keep moving in the forward direction, slowly but surely. Your individual evolution is almost exactly like this snail-paced automatic car. Even if you don't put any conscious efforts, the evolution will keep happening on its own but at a very slow, lazy, lethargic pace. The exciting fact is that in the same automatic car, the manufacturer has also kept a turbo gear or a sports gear. With skilful use of the available instruments of accelerator, break and steering wheel, etc., an expert driver can cover long distances in a very short time. Similarly, through *optimum utilization* of the instruments given to you by the nature of body-breath-mind-intellect-memory and ego; through your *Committed Skilful Efforts* you have the opportunity of tremendously accelerating the process of evolution of your own consciousness.

This incessant process of evolution seems to have these extremely important, almost inevitable two transformative steps:

1. Recognizing and releasing negative emotions, binding perspectives and harmful tendencies
2. Regular invocation of life-beautifying flavours

The first step involves recognizing and releasing your harmful tendencies, becoming free of all the binding, limiting, detrimental *reverse gears*. Just like a surgeon uses an MRI (magnetic resonance imaging) machine to scan and locate tumours and skilfully removes them for the complete healing of the body. As we have discussed earlier, the development, the progress of the individual consciousness is a very technical process. As a soul goes through its individual lives, through different events, a variety of *bhavas*, flavours, get triggered in its consciousness. Sometimes knowingly, sometimes unknowingly, sometimes voluntarily, sometimes involuntarily, sometimes deliberately, sometimes accidentally, whichever flavour, whichever emotion gets triggered repeatedly, forms its own tendency, its vrutti, some harmful tendencies, klisht vruttis, some harmless tendencies, aklisht vruttis. Here at this juncture, we are about to plunge into the exploration of your harmful tendencies. Once you recognize them and understand their detrimental effects on your personal life, an instinctive desire to be free from them arises. *In the realm of consciousness, there is a rule: your willingness to be free is your qualification to be free. The intensity of your will to be free determines how quickly you will be free.*

In the second step, as your individual consciousness gradually attains freedom from its negative tendencies, with the reverse gears getting disengaged on a regular basis and a free, neutral platform getting established, it is time for you to take this transformative step: committedly, resiliently and courageously invoking life-transforming flavours and enhancing energy levels to expand the consciousness to experience oneness with the Brahman. We will address this most benevolent subject a little later in the book.

II. Minute details of harmful tendencies: Shadripus, the six enemies of your consciousness and their dangerous influence on your life

For millennia, in the eastern part of the world, the rishis, the saints, the enlightened masters, have carried out an extremely minute study of the consciousness and have given very specific guidelines to protect the individual consciousness from 'unnecessary trouble'. What we are about to discuss is one such marvel from the treasure of spiritual exploration. The ancient seers shortlisted the activities which cause dramatic contraction of consciousness, resulting in a drastic drop in happiness, positiveness and purity. They called these activities the *shadripus*, the six enemies of the consciousness, six reverse gears in the process of evolution:

1. *Kaam* – Lust
2. *Krodh* – Anger
3. *Lobh* – Greed
4. *Moh* – Attachment/infatuation
5. *Madh* – Flavours of ego
6. *Matsar* – Jealousy

Before we begin this intense personal exploration, I want to take this opportunity to appreciate the sensitivity with which this delicate and volatile subject has been handled by the rishis. Very firmly they proclaimed that these are 'harmful' tendencies, not 'wrong' or 'bad' tendencies. If someone indulges in these detrimental patterns, their energy drops temporarily, they lose their vitality and their process of evolution slows down or goes into the reverse gear for a while. But the person doesn't become a wrong or bad person. The basic nature of truth, consciousness, bliss still remains. Once again, I invite you to courageously look at your own life, apply the student's formula of Shravan-Manan-Nidhidhyas: receiving open-heartedly, contemplating how these activities are influencing your own life and courageously committing yourself to making your mind free from them for this knowledge to become a part of your life. As soon as the will to be free arises in you, you will see, instantaneously, the process of freedom begins.

1) Kaam (Lust)

Throughout centuries, many learned ones have avoided talking about this taboo subject. On the one hand, this ancient, long-standing tendency has served the purpose of procreation and progeny. Souls from all the yonis have indulged in this basic instinct of *kamavasana*—lust for the process of birth and death to continue. On the other hand, excessive indulgence in this highest sensory pleasure can cause tremendous drop in personal energy levels. Let us look at the facts scientifically, taking the reference of our own life. Among the five senses of watching, listening, smelling, tasting and touching, sex, intercourse, masturbation, orgasm, is the highest pleasurable experience. But see how extremely short-lived it is. As the pleasure builds up and in just a few minutes reaches its crescendo, observe what happens immediately after the pinnacle is crossed. Your energy drops, you feel tired; your awareness, your agility and your pleasantness get drained; your consciousness contracts.

One more interesting observation from the perspective of Ayurveda, the Vedic science of physical, mental, emotional, intellectual and spiritual well-being: In this ancient science, the seers have proclaimed that various functions of all the physiological systems of the human body are carried out by these seven components, the *Saptadhatu*:

1. *Rasa* (bodily fluids)
2. *Rakta* (blood)
3. *Mamsa* (muscular tissue)
4. *Medas* (adipose tissue)
5. *Asthi* (bones)
6. *Majja* (bone marrow and nervous tissue)
7. *Shukra* (generative tissue, including semen and ovum constituents)

Since it is your own consciousness that creates your body, even to create these *dhatus* or components your own energy is utilized. The amount of energy (shakti) required to create a particular dhatu depends on their functions and individual potencies. Of the seven dhatus, the *shukra* dhatu is the most potent. In men it is the semen, which contains sperm; in women it is the vaginal fluid, including the ovum. The shukra dhatu has the inherent capacity to create a whole new physical body by itself. Hence it takes a tremendous amount of shakti, prana, to create this dhatu. You will be astonished to know how extraordinarily potent the shukra dhatu is. The amount of energy-prana-shakti required to create just one droplet of the shukra dhatu is equivalent to the amount of energy required to create thousands of droplets of blood. The shukra dhatu is that much potent, that much powerful, that much alive.

The natural design of the body is such that as soon as any of these dhatus are used, the whole body gets engaged in the process of manufacturing and replenishing that particular dhatu. For example, if blood is lost from the body because of some reason, this extremely intelligent mechanism gets into the overdrive mode to create and replenish blood. Let us open-heartedly translate this understanding of the dhatus and their potencies with reference to sexual activity. Just for a few minutes of sexual pleasure, if you continuously lose this intensely powerful and potent shukra dhatu, either through intercourse or through masturbation, your whole experience of life takes a big hit. Rather than getting utilized in the enhancement of individual consciousness, your life force is constantly in an emergency-supply mode, for replenishing the shukra dhatu. Your effulgence, your valour, your brightness, your brilliance, your sharpness, your radiance—all of it goes down the drain. You would have noticed that those who repetitively indulge in sexual activities, their skin looks dry, flaky and lustreless, almost dark; whereas those who committedly refrain from this temporary pleasure look bright and vibrant with a radiant glow. Hence in every spiritual path, sooner or later, the discipline of celibacy (*brahmacharya*) is strongly recommended. Those who are interested in spiritual upliftment, in exploring the infinite potential of the consciousness, should acquire the personal discipline of non-indulgence in sexual activity. You can start with self-restraint for a few months in the beginning. As the rishis say, 'भोग के तृप्ति नहीं . . . भाग के मुक्ति नहीं . . . No amount of indulgence is going to satisfy this incessant craving.' As you indulge in it more and more, the tendency of lust gets stronger and stronger in you. On the other hand, resisting the temptation is not going to set the mind free from this habit of lust. A little later in the book, we will discuss the middle path, the path of surrender. Neither will we indulge, nor will we resist. We will learn to let go, surrender, release, delete . . . And be free, once and for all.

2) Krodh (Anger)

Earlier in the book, while describing the intimidating/ aggressive flavour of the ego, we touched this explosive subject. Let's now look at the phenomenon of anger scientifically. In this event-by-event flow of life, when something goes wrong, when somebody says something or does something that is against your wish, and some desire or expectation of yours does not get fulfilled, the first thing that happens is a little tightness in your individual consciousness, in the form of dislike, disagreement or resentment. If this tightness, this resistance is not dropped using a sharp awareness, it consolidates into complaint or blame. And if at this stage, these intense emotions are not released, they culminate into anger. Usually, when you get angry you want to express it in words and blast someone. If you don't get that chance, it can escalate right up to the level of hatred. From dislike to complaint to anger to hatred—all of this is described by the ancient seers in one word, krodh. It scorches your individual consciousness, like a blowtorch, and eventually burns away the beautiful flavours of belongingness, love and harmony in the collective consciousness too.

In Bhagavad Gita, Lord Krishna proclaims:

ध्यायतो विषयान्पुंसः संगस्तेषूपजायते ।
संगात्संजायते कामः कामात्क्रोधोऽभिजायते ।।
क्रोधाद्भवति सम्मोहः सम्मोहात्स्मृतिविभ्रमः ।
स्मृतिभ्रंशाद् बुद्धिनाशो बुद्धिनाशात्प्रणश्यति ।।

When a person repetitively indulges in sensory pleasures, a sense of attachment with the pleasures arises. From attachment, desire is born; and from unfulfilled desires, anger is generated. When this hypnotizing anger engulfs the human mind, even the memory of who you are, who you are getting angry with, who is observing you, etc., is completely lost. This results in a dramatic decline in your basic intelligence, your vivek (wisdom). And as this common sense takes a hit, it eventually leads to a drastic drop in the stature of the soul, the stage of evolution. The purity and integrity of the individual consciousness is compromised. Not only does this explosive tendency of anger scorches your own consciousness, it also burns away harmony and beauty from the collective consciousness. At home, in the office or in a group of friends, many times you would have noticed that in a harmonious, free-flowing, relaxed atmosphere, just one person's anger can make the whole collective atmosphere tight, vicious and full of fire. In the current stage of *kaliyuga*, when this minute, sensitive, delicate understanding of the consciousness is at its lowest level, the use of anger and aggression to get some work done is perceived to be almost like a virtue. Using extreme kutarkas (twisted logic), people justify their anger and intimidation. The more they justify it, the more intense their anger grows. Like in the case of alcoholics or drug addicts, they need stronger and stronger doses to get the same intoxication, in the case of anger, you will need harsher and harsher expressions to create the same effect on people, but in that process, your individual consciousness becomes more and more hard, coarse and shrill.

As the Buddha says, '*Holding on to anger is like holding a red-hot coal in your hand, waiting to throw it at someone, but while you are waiting, who is getting burnt?*'

Sometimes patience looks like a waste of time but from the perspective of purity of consciousness, impatience leads to feverishness, restlessness, frustration and anger. Whereas patience is a long-term investment, giving you extraordinary returns of love, trust and harmony.

3) Lobh (Greed) and 4) Moh (Attachment)

Through centuries, in all the cultures of the world, these two harmful tendencies of the consciousness have been vastly criticized, condemned and ridiculed. History is a witness: whenever lobh (greed and hoarding) or moh (infatuation, delusion, attachment) has gripped the human mind, it has inevitably led to corruption, unethical, immoral indulgences, leading to war and the eventual destruction of even the most powerful civilizations. Search of happiness, seeking joy, looking for pleasure has always been a very natural, very spontaneous, almost instinctive trait of the mind. As we have discussed before in the book, Happiness-Sukh-Ananda is a driving force behind most of the activities of people. The trouble begins when you start looking for happiness in the *wrong place*. Lobh-greed and moh-attachment are included in the list of shadripus, the six enemies of the consciousness, because of a dangerous common factor. They give you the illusion that the source of your joy, happiness, sukh, is somewhere out there. When lobh is predominant, you attach your sukh with *vastu* and *paristhiti* (things and situations). *'Yeh dil maange more'* is the formula. Wanting more and more of the worldly possessions, from money to car to gold to clothes to jewellery to property, believing blindly that they will give you satisfaction, fulfilment and security.

But look at this peculiar phenomenon: till the time you get your hands on them possess them, look how lucrative and attractive these items appear to you but as soon as you possess them, they completely lose their charm. Till the time a piece of jewellery, a dress is in the showroom, look how it lures your mind, but as soon as you bring it home, it loses its significance. One more item gets added to the already overflowing wardrobe. Look how important it is for you to attain the higher post in your company or organization but as soon as you reach there, 'poof' . . . the soap bubble bursts. Look at how your mind hankers for bigger, better, costlier things. But look at what happens the moment you possess them. As lobh (greed) erroneously attaches happiness and success to physical articles and social stature, moha attaches joy and security with people. Look how sure and certain people are that everything will be okay once they get married. Look how much of dependence people have on each other, look how strongly people believe that their security depends on their relationships. But let us apply a reality check to this delusion. One wrong incident, one intense negative emotion, one bout of distrust, and this illusory sense of togetherness and security evaporates into thin air. Look at the drama of relationships. Every individual soul is passing through its own journey. Having travelled through millions of lifetimes as we took this current human body, almost accidentally, we found ourselves connected to each other in various relationships.

Somebody became your father, somebody your mother, your brother, your sister, your friend, your husband or wife, your child and so on. And as one day this body will be dropped, each one of us would continue onwards on our own individual journeys. In this lifetime, moh creates an illusion of togetherness, dependence, bondage and security. Vivek, intelligence, wisdom, is nothing but searching for bliss in the *right place*. Avivek, *agyaan*, non-intelligence, lack of wisdom, is to look for joy where it is not; searching for happiness in the *wrong place*. In this two-sectioned phenomenon of life, the outer world of people-things-situations gives you an illusion of happiness, success and security created by greed and attachment (lobh and moh) whereas the inner world, your personal consciousness is a reservoir of Ananda, where a precious treasure of bliss is waiting to be unearthed. Spirituality, swadhyay, self-exploration, is nothing but the quest to find the key to this *infinite treasure chest* within. Those who have not explored the consciousness and hence not understood this subtle reality, tend to fall for the untruth, for the illusions of greed and attachments.

5) Madh (Ego)

This madh, this I-ness, this ego is the most dangerous enemy of them all. A very detailed explanation of this ego is already given earlier in the book. I recommend that you please refer to it once again in the context of the six enemies, the shadripus. Once you understand and identify the flavours of ego that frequently haunt you, half the job is already done. One example will explain this better. Imagine you've entered an extremely dark room with zero visibility around you. While you are looking for the light switch to turn on, you accidentally catch a hanging rope. You think the rope is a good support while you are still fumbling for the switch. But as you find the light switch and turn it on, to your shock, you realize it is not a rope you are holding on to, it is a snake or a cobra. What will you do? In that moment do you need to intellectualize that *this is a poisonous snake?* '*It will bite me. The poison will spread. It might kill me,* etc.' What do you instinctively do? You let go of the snake, isn't it? Similarly, just the identification of the flavours of the ego is good enough for you to want to drop them. The awareness itself creates a platform for the desire to be free to arise.

Hence the learned rishis have proclaimed, '*The ego can survive only in the darkness of agyaan (unawareness). In the light of knowledge and awareness the ego disappears.*' In your own life, once you become aware that your superiority-complex ego has haunted you in some relationship, the awareness itself helps you to dissolve the superiority and judgemental attitude and become humble, soft and open with them. Once you recognize how the victim ego destroys your strength and makes you a cribbing runt, that recognition itself starts the process of dissolving the ego and being free from it. In this rollercoaster ride called life, whenever untoward situations trigger these different flavours of the ego, observe what they do to your perception, observation and expression. Look at how they colour your vision, how they restrict your response to the need of the moment. Without these flavours of the ego, how easy and effortless it would be for you to handle the challenges of life, the difficult situations in relationships and to maintain harmony in your inner world as well as your outer world. Hence the learned ones proclaimed, *'The ego is the only reason behind any misery in your life.'*

6) Matsar (Jealousy)

Last but not the least, let us not underestimate the destructive power of this subtle and slimy emotion. When matsar, *irsha*, jealousy, envy, gets triggered in you, look what all dangerous games it makes you play. When you see someone achieving something, being successful or being praised for their goodness, strengths and virtues, it triggers a sense of lack, *abhava*, in you. You feel that particular strength and quality is missing in your life. You feel you are not good enough. A sense of competition and contest to the level of conflict makes you want to show off. Makes you want to be one up, makes you find faults with them. When you are gripped by matsar, jealousy, often the feeling is not, *'why do they have it'*. Mostly it is, *'I don't have it'*, *'I am lacking in it'*. If this feeling of lack, leading to inferiority complex, is not identified and dropped, it inevitably leads you to fault-finding. You will look for people who talk negative or complain about the one you are jealous of. If something wrong or harmful happens to them, you feel demonic pleasure, *rakshashi sukh*. Hence, the learned ones have compared jealousy and envy to a poisonous snake. Once its venom spreads into the blood, your righteousness, correctness, purity and Dharma—your commitment to the full blossoming of your consciousness—all of it goes down the drain. Courageously and non-defensively look at the relationships of your life. Identify the people you are jealous of. When you feel jealous and a sense of lack and smallness gets triggered in you, look how badly you want them to fail and falter. Look how hard you try to convince others how wrong and bad they are! See how cunning, slimy, manipulative and impure that makes you feel. Some very effective, powerful techniques are available for you if you wish to drop the flavour of jealousy and stop this breakneck decline of your integrity and purity. Remember: 'Your desire to be free is your qualification to be free.' So the more you justify, hide, deny jealousy, the more it will stay with you. Your mind. Your life. Your choices. Your responsibility.

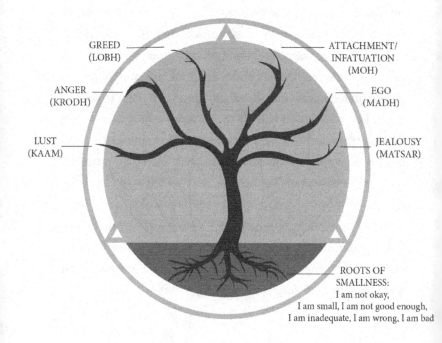

GREED
(LOBH)

ATTACHMENT/
INFATUATION
(MOH)

ANGER
(KRODH)

EGO
(MADH)

LUST
(KAAM)

JEALOUSY
(MATSAR)

ROOTS OF
SMALLNESS:
I am not okay,
I am small, I am not good enough,
I am inadequate, I am wrong, I am bad

The Tree of Shadripu

III. *Swadhyay* – Self-exploration – Optimizing your role in the game of life

At this juncture in the book, it is necessary to understand the importance of swadhyay, self-exploration. The basis of swadhyay lies in recognizing and acknowledging your own role in the game of life. Nature has bestowed enormous abilities on the individual consciousness. These inner powers, when put to use, can create marvellous results in your own life. A thorough understanding of these subtle inner strengths and their skilful utilization for the benevolence of your own life is part of swadhyay.

As discussed before, your individual life is unfolding in your inner world every moment. The collective consciousness of people, things and situations is just an instrument that triggers different flavours, different bhavas, different tendencies in you. Whichever flavour gets invoked in you vastly determines the experience and the quality of your life for that moment. Having recognized and acknowledged this subtle truth, let's now explore some of the inner powers of your consciousness.

1) Nature has already given you the ability to invoke any flavour that you want to invoke, whenever and wherever you want, at will, on demand. In any moment of your life, in any kind of situation, you have the freedom to bring up anything you want, in your own consciousness. To get first-hand experience of this inner power, let us try a practical process. Right now, while you are reading this book, try and invoke love in your

consciousness, and you will feel that beautiful flavour of love getting triggered in you. Try and invoke enthusiasm right now, and you will actually feel enthusiastic. Try to bring up valour and patriotism right now and at this very moment you can roar like a lion! The creator has bestowed this power on everyone: the ability to invoke any bhava at will, on demand, whenever and wherever you want. Try and experiment with this process of invocation in different situations, different surroundings with different people around you.

2) The second fantastic ability each one of us has is to be able to drop anything from our consciousness. If some negative, harmful, restrictive flavour comes up in you, you have the complete freedom to let it go, release it, drop it and free your consciousness from it, any moment you want. Even if you have held on to some negative emotion for a long time and suddenly you want to drop it, you are free to let go of it, right now. A little later in the book, we shall discuss technical ways of freeing your mind from anything and everything that you want to be free from.

3) The third extraordinary ability of the human consciousness: whichever flavour comes up in you recurrently, forms its own tendency, its own habit, in your consciousness. If you keep invoking beautiful flavours—like love, enthusiasm, compassion—on a regular basis, your consciousness soon gets habituated to those beautiful flavours and the autopilot takes over. Exactly the opposite of that is also true; if because of your past indulgences in harmful flavours, their tendencies have formed in you, and you committedly and regularly keep

dropping them, slowly but surely, you will get free from them. The human consciousness is naturally designed to generate the tendencies as well as to release the tendencies at will, on demand. Whichever tendency prevails in you, profoundly influences the experience of your life. Each individual soul is a reservoir of these marvellous strengths. *'Inherently, you already have all the powers necessary to create the life that you want. You are not designed to be a slave of circumstances; you are designed to be the master of situations.'*

Understanding the play of your own consciousness and exploring your true nature, what you really are, is also a part of swadhyay. In this courageous endeavour of self-exploration, the swadhyay, this formula will help you tremendously: no guilt, no defence. While delving into deeper truths and identifying your role in the game of life, specifically when your harmful tendencies are getting exposed, these two flavours of the ego, guilt and defence, are extremely detrimental. As you learn to recognize your own contribution in this event-by-event phenomenon of life and realize your own mistakes, these two arc the most common, most frequent, most general reactions. Those who are sincere tend to feel guilty, regretful, and tend to blame themselves; while those who are flamboyant, arrogant and egoistic tend to defend, justify or deny everything as soon as their role in the game of life is exposed. When you feel guilty, your shakti, your resilience, your commitment to be free is broken down. When you feel defensive, your attention and intention are aimed more towards justifying your shortcomings rather than towards being free. What we need is the middle path between these two extremes. What we need is the student formula: Shravan-Manan-Nidhidhyas. To further break down the process of swadhyay, let us understand these three components:

1. Identifying the tendencies
2. Recognizing the conversations
3. Recognizing the platform/base

1) Identifying the tendencies

In this event-by-event phenomenon of life, with different people, with different situations, learn to recognize the tendencies that are getting triggered in you. If a particular emotion or flavour of ego is getting triggered in you recurrently, if it is surfacing almost involuntarily, by default, it's a sign that this particular emotion is definitely becoming a tendency. These tendencies vastly influence the experience and quality of your life. Identifying the tendency is the first most necessary step towards being free from it.

2) Recognizing your conversations

In any aspect of your life—the people-situations-things in your outer world or the manasa-vacha-karmana of your inner world—*your conversations are creating your own reality*. I like this word 'conversation'. When I say 'conversation', I am including your thoughts, emotions, memories, judgements, likes-dislikes, rights-wrongs, and your beliefs in this one word 'conversation'. Look at this fantastic phenomenon. Whatever you are 'conversing' about a person or a situation vastly influences your experience with them. Isn't it? From important relationships, to God, to spirituality, even about yourself, your conversations are creating your own reality. I am not saying that your conversations are wrong or incorrect, or that you should not have these conversations. All I am saying is, your conversations are based on your past experiences. And they vastly influence your experience of people-situations-things, even your experience of yourself. I am saying that your life occurs in your conversations!

I invite you for a courageous expedition of your inner world, where your conversations are influencing your experience. Ask yourself these three simple yet profound questions:

(i)   Are your conversations real?
(ii)   Are your conversations forwarding your life?
(iii) Are you courageous and free enough to drop the undesirable conversations?

(i) Are your conversations real?

In any aspect of your life, your past experiences have caused your beliefs, emotions, memories and conversations. At times, people around you share their experiences with you and consciously or unconsciously you agree with them, believe in them and include their opinions in your own conversations. Many times you will notice that you often believe in something not because of your own experiences but because your family, society, the world has believed in it. Though you did not have a personal experience, you gave consent, an agreement and allowed someone's opinion to become your conversation, your reality. I am saying, courageously pass your conversations through a *reality check*. Verify their validity, filter truth from untruth, real from unreal. You may be surprised to realize how deeply 'unrealness' has coloured your mind and influenced the decisions that have given a direction to your life. An interesting process: I want to invite you to sit with yourself, with your eyes closed, and mentally make a list of all the important people and aspects of your life, and one after the other check your conversations, your beliefs about them. Are your conversations real? Are they complete truth or have you experienced only a few facets of the diamond and believed the whole diamond to be like that? *Check your conversations about yourself as well. Are you sure you are what you have believed yourself to be?* Check your conversations about money or family or God. Is there a possibility that half-truths and limited understanding have influenced your conversations? Whatever you have believed has influenced your choices, your decisions, which in turn have given a direction to your life. In short, my first question is, '*Are your conversations real?*'

(ii) Are your conversations forwarding your life?

After you have gone through the reality check and filtered the truth from untruth, this second question will open a deeper layer of swadhyay. Whatever you are conversing about any person or about any situation, please ask yourself these questions:

- Is your conversation contracting your consciousness or leading to the blossoming of your heart?
- Is it creating bondage or is it setting you free?
- Is it harmful for your life or is it beneficial?
- Is it reversing the process of evolution or is it accelerating the full blossoming of your consciousness?
- Is it Dharma or is it Adharma ?

Having understood the fact that in any aspect of your life your reality occurs in your conversations, you must realize that many of your conversations may not be complete truths (*purna satya*). That is when this second question of swadhyay becomes so important, so relevant, almost inevitable for the seeker of truth. In life, it is up to you to decide which thought or emotion is worth keeping and which isn't, which belief is beneficial and which one is harmful, which decision to keep and which one to drop. Even if something appears very real, if it is damaging your consciousness, not letting you be free, becoming a hindrance in the process of full blossoming, I am saying, what is the point in holding on to it?

(iii) Are you courageous and free enough to drop undesirable conversations?

Finally, it boils down to this intense question. As discussed earlier, *your life, your mind, your choices are your own responsibility.* In this game of life, each individual soul is experiencing its own life, immensely influenced by the conversations it has managed to gather. *Now that we have explored that every soul is free and able to invoke any flavour at will and is also capable of dropping any flavour whenever it wants, the stage has come to ask this direct, intense, almost challenging question to yourself: Are you free enough, committed enough, courageous enough, to drop the negative, to release the bondage, to disengage the reverse gears?* Most of the time, the identification of a negative tendency or a harmful conversation instinctively invokes a desire to be free from it, because the basic nature of the consciousness is of truth, energy and bliss. The natural instinct to be free from untruth and unhappiness is almost ingrained in the consciousness. But sometimes, in spite of knowing how harmful a tendency is, how damaging a conversation is, you are not free enough to drop them because you feel, '*How can I suddenly drop something which I have held on to and believed in for so long? Now if I drop it, it will directly mean I was wrong all this while.*' Your lack of courage, your wanting to blame others because of your victim consciousness, your need to justify your judgements, and sometimes sheer lethargy and laziness obstruct you from dropping, releasing, deleting the negative. I am saying, once you learn the skill to let go, nothing in the world can bother you for long and damage your effective decision-making.

3) Recognizing the platform/base

At this juncture, I invite you to further sharpen your awareness. In the process of swadhyay, this is the deepest and subtle-most layer: recognizing the platform, the base, the grounds on which your tendencies and your conversations are held and supported. Look at the experience of your life. Look at how people become invisible platforms for the strengths or weaknesses to get triggered in each other. If you are able to sensitively identify this abstract reality, you will see that some people, with their presence, unconsciously support you in activities like shopping, movies, eating junk food, etc., whereas some others, just by their mere presence, guide you towards meditation, prayers, higher evolution, away from indulgences in temporary and sensory pleasures. Look at the important relationships of your life. Each one of them is instrumental in triggering different flavours, different tendencies, different conversations in you. Somebody always becomes a platform, a base where love is triggered in you; whereas someone else's presence invokes naughtiness, fun, cheeky flavours in you. Some people by their mere presence invoke deeper truths and swadhyay for you, whereas someone else always breaks your resolve to meditate. Someone with their influence on you, subconsciously protects you from the shadripus; whereas someone else, unknowingly, becomes an excuse for you to indulge in these harmful activities. Someone becomes a base of Dharma for you, while someone else unconsciously creates a ground for Adharma. In the process of evolution, each individual soul has its own flavours of consciousness. This *unseen presence* becomes an invisible platform for other souls around them to experience the same flavours. Some people, because of their extreme devotion, become a silent platform for others around them to get a glimpse of devotion. Some with their celebratory enthusiasm, invoke enthusiasm around them. Someone with extreme depths of truth causes thousands around them to find their own truth. I am saying, sometimes *people* become invisible platforms for each other's tendencies and conversations to be supported. Whereas at other times, *intense events* of the past become invisible base for conversations, beliefs and tendencies to be held in your consciousness. Something drastic happened that instigated you to take some strong decisions, which became a turning point in shaping your life, for it to be where it is today. You will see, the decision taken in that intense event is still becoming a platform that supports your tendencies, conversations and decisions even today. *Sometimes beneficial, sometimes harmful, sometimes blossoming, sometimes restricting—all your tendencies have an invisible base or a platform, either of people or of past events, that hold your tendencies or your conversations in your consciousness.* In the process of swadhyay, for knowing the complete truth, for viewing the whole diamond with all its facets, recognizing this unseen, invisible platform, the base, the launch pad, is almost unavoidable. For anything and everything to be what it is today, some event in the past would have become the platform. If you want to understand someone's behaviour, you will also have to sensitively understand their culture, their tradition, their way of life. If some tendency or conversation needs to be released and dropped completely from your consciousness, you will also need to address the justifying, validating ground that unconsciously supports that tendency or conversation.

Having recognized and acknowledged this subtle reality, it's time to internalize this knowledge in your own life. Look at all the harmful tendencies and detrimental conversations you want to be free from and identify who and what has become a platform, a base, an invisible ground, on which they are being supported. There is only one catch here. As you open up this deeper layer of truth, beware of your victim ego and defensive tendency. Instead of recognizing and committing to be free, this poor-me attitude can start its blame game all over again and justify your own shortcomings.

In the next chapter, we will understand how to be free from the undesirable tendencies, conversations and platforms.

Worksheet

Make a note of all the 'pearls of wisdom' that you would like to retain from this chapter for your future reference

....

....

....

....

....

....

....

....

....

....

....

....

....

....

....

....

....

....

....

....

....

....

Enlist the tendencies among the shadripus, the six enemies, and their influence on various aspects of your life

....
....
....
....
....
....
....
....
....
....
....
....
....
....
....
....
....
....
....
....
....
....
....
....
....
....
....
....

Make a list of the conversations and platforms supporting the harmful tendencies
(Take your own time. Minute and detailed description will help you.)

....
....
....
....
....
....
....
....
....
....
....
....
....
....
....
....
....
....
....
....
....
....

Step Four

Being Free from All Bondages, Negativities and Harmful Tendencies

At this juncture, now that we have identified the bad guys, the villains, the shadripus, understood the unrealness of the *conversations* and their profound influence on our lives, and explored the deeper layer of swadhyay to recognize the base and the platform, it's time to look for solutions. It's time to find ways to be free. It's time to delete the infected, infested, corrupted folders.

As discussed before, nature, Brahman, the universe, has bestowed limitless abilities on the human consciousness. Among many such siddhis is the ability to let go of *anything* that you want to drop from your inner world, at will, on demand, whenever you want. You can use this transformative ability of the human mind to release any thoughts, emotions, memories, judgements, likes or dislikes, rights or wrongs, harmful tendencies, any flavour of ego, any conversations or platforms, and be completely free from them. If I use computer terminology here, every relationship, every event, every tendency is like a folder; and memories, impressions, likes or dislikes, thoughts or emotions, judgements or labels are like the files stored in them. When we visit any website, the cookies and temporary files get automatically downloaded on the hard disk. Similarly, as we go through different situations in life, various impressions, emotions, judgements and past experiences get accumulated within us, almost involuntarily, by default. If the hard disk of a computer has the ability to collect data and store it, it can also delete the data and erase the history completely, when given the command to do so. Similarly, whatever impressions, tendencies, judgements, labels or flavours of ego are accumulated throughout lifetimes in the conscious and subconscious levels of your memory, using your attention as the cursor to open the folders and the outgoing breath as the delete button, you can let go of anything and everything that you want to be free from.

The incoming breath energizes the body, provides vital force and supports the soul so that it continues to live in the physical form; the outgoing breath removes impurities from the body and empties your individual consciousness. The secret is, the more empty, the more free the mind is, the more happy it is and more available it is to do anything that you want to do with it. It is very similar to how a vacuum cleaner operates. Once you connect the vacuum cleaner to the power source and switch the machine on, you don't attend to the machine too much. Your whole focus is on the area, the corner, the crevice that needs cleaning. Wherever you take the nozzle of the vacuum cleaner, the machine will suck the dust away from there. Isn't it? Similarly, you take your attention to anything you want to be free from and visualize that you are putting your thoughts, emotions, memories, judgements, etc., into the outgoing breath and your exhalation is taking it out of your inner world and releasing it into space. Your mind, your attention, is like the nozzle of a vacuum cleaner and your outgoing breath is the machine that sucks the dust away. *In the process of letting go, releasing or deleting, your willingness to be free, your readiness to let go and surrender is the key. Sometimes the victim ego does not allow you to be in the frame of mind to drop the negative emotions, because it is not interested in letting go of the garbage and being free. It thrives on blaming others so that it can pity itself. Right now, we are not interested in this stupid ego.*

With a clear objective of attaining freedom, you can learn to use the outgoing breath and your ability to let go of anything and everything you want—at will, on demand. It is a very subtle, sensitive, skilful way. Withdraw your mind from the outer world, being fully with yourself, whatever comes up in your consciousness, whichever folder opens up, with mindful awareness when you simply '*be with it*', all the impressions, tendencies, emotions and conversations from the consciousness get lifted away. Ours is a very sensitive middle path: neither do we resist any emotion or sensation, nor do we indulge in it. These negative emotions are not your nature. The basic nature of consciousness is of emptiness. When your intention is of letting go, whatever negativity comes up in your awareness gets lifted off. The skill is to withdraw from the outer world and just be with it, without resisting it, let the negativity get released. Whatever you want to be free from, don't be in a hurry to get rid of it. Let it take its own time. Wait for it to completely get deleted. Remember, if the file or folder is big, it will take that much more time to delete it. The more empty the consciousness is, the more happy and more available it is.

Sudarshan Kriya, taught in the Art of Living Happiness Program, is one such transformative breathing technique that has helped millions of people the world over to free their minds from the klisht vruttis, harmful tendencies, limiting conversations and past impressions. Once you learn this powerful process that you can practice every day, two wonderful things happen:

1. The mind becomes free, happy and focused.
2. Your energy levels are dramatically enhanced.

With heightened shakti and a pure, positive mind, you are able to effortlessly handle the challenges of your life. Once you learn to drop anything at will, you will realize that even when you remember the people you were unhappy with, your mind does not feel the same unpleasantness. If you revisit the events or situations of the past that have always triggered negative emotions in you, you will find your mind relieved of its old 'tightness'. At the experiential level, if you feel freer, lighter, happier and purer, having dropped the unnecessary baggage of the past, of negative tendencies, conversations and platforms, this process of letting go, surrendering, deleting is working for you. If you recollect your mistakes that always made you feel guilty, once you drop the guilt, the burden of self-blame gets lifted off your conscience. When you just be with yourself and observe your inner world, you will be surprised to see what all this mind has accumulated through lifetimes. Something went wrong and the judgement stayed on. Something went against your wish and the blame lingered on. A small mistake by you and the guilt is retained. Whichever flavour of the ego got triggered in you recurrently, it formed its own tendencies, habits, conversations. Many times you will notice that while you don't even remember the events, the unpleasant flavours have stayed on.

There is another way of dealing with your harmful tendencies while you are operating in the world: it's a two-step process. The first step is to observe whatever is happening within you and be a witness, moment to moment to moment. The second step is to let go, release, surrender. As we know, different people, things and situations of the outer world manage to trigger different emotions, flavours, bhavas in you. The discipline of being a witness gives you the opportunity of practising the power of your mind to let go while you are at work, dealing with different aspects of your life, moment to moment. This witnessing and letting go, gives you an opportunity to take responsibility for the pleasantness, positiveness and purity of your inner world at will, on demand, whenever and wherever you want.

The first step is to be a witness to what is happening in your inner world and to learn to *Observe* your tendencies, conversations and platforms. The second step is to let go, release, delete, *Surrender*, using the outgoing breath. With different people, in different situations, because of the already formed tendencies, different emotions, bhavas get triggered in you. As you learn to observe whatever is happening within you, you get the choice, the freedom to drop any negative thought, harmful emotion, detrimental perspective, and to not let it influence your openness and positiveness. Suddenly you will realize that you are no more a slave of your tendencies. Even if someone is behaving very badly or wrongly with you, and you are beginning to feel upset, you can, with sheer commitment and skill, prevent your mind from being influenced by them. Even in the most vicious and challenging situations at home or at work, when you are about to react strongly and hit back, with the practice of being in the *sakshi bhav*, witness consciousness, rather than getting carried away by the flow of events you can maintain equilibrium and harmony in your inner world. If negativity builds up in you, you react. When you keep releasing the tightness and maintain your inner harmony, you sensitively respond to the need of the moment and make things better. Isn't it?

In the beginning, this discipline of being a witness and of surrendering might appear to be a *very difficult job*. But as you practise it regularly, the benefits and results will inspire you to practise it more and more, and it will get easier and easier for you. Very soon, you will get habituated to it. People of low intelligence sometimes fall for the thought '*Oh, it is so difficult*' and drop the process; whereas people with higher intelligence say, '*It appears to be difficult but I see its value. Let me commit myself to practising it.*' As they say, practice makes a man perfect. Commit yourself to the practice of being a witness of your inner world and to the practice of letting go of the unpleasantness, negativities and harmful tendencies, till this skill becomes a part of your nature and autopilot takes over. With the three powerful instruments of your attention, your outgoing breath and your ability to let go, the process of becoming free has these two components. On the one hand, you will need to learn to sit with yourself with your eyes closed, withdraw your mind from the world, open different folders in your consciousness and delete the infested, infected files. On the other hand, while you are operating in the world, tackling different challenges, you do not have the privilege of closing your eyes. In those moments, observing and surrendering will help you immensely.

An example will explain these processes better. Imagine a well full of water, where leaves, flowers, twigs from the surrounding vegetation have fallen on the surface of the water. If you want to clean the surface, all you need is a cleaning net. However, if you want to remove the mud that has accumulated underneath, you will need to use a powerful pump and a suction pipe that reaches the bottom of the well to suck the mud and the debris away. This discipline of witnessing and letting go is like using the cleaning net to remove the twigs and leaves from the surface of the water; whereas the discipline of sitting with yourself, withdrawing the mind from the world, diving deep within (Sudarshan Kriya and meditation), is very much like using the suction pump. It helps you to open deeper layers of your consciousness to remove accumulated tendencies, conversations and platforms over lifetimes.

Worksheet

Make a note of all the 'pearls of wisdom' that you would like to retain from this chapter for your future reference

....
....
....
....
....
....
....
....
....

Make your own daily schedule of practising this process of being a witness and surrendering harmful tendencies, restricting conversations and detrimental platforms

....
....
....
....
....
....
....
....

Step Five

Optimizing the Golden Opportunity of Being in the Human Body

Having covered a lot of topics related to the rules and laws of the universal consciousness, and having discussed the play of the soul, the individual consciousness, we have now reached a pivotal point in this book. On the one hand, the existence of the individual soul seems so trivial, so irrelevant, insignificant in this boundless, limitless, infinite creation, like a small, tiny, minuscule bubble in the ocean. On the other hand, we are also exploring how infinitely powerful each individual soul is. On the one hand, we are exploring the *Science of Being*, whereby we comprehend the technical laws, rules and principles according to which universal existence operates. On the other hand, we are also sensitively learning the *Art of Living*, the skilful manoeuvring, optimum utilization of your inner resources to understand the infinite potential of the human consciousness and to explore the divinity within.

I. The three precious instruments of your life:
   Time – Energy – Mind

At this point, I want to reveal a precious aspect of the truth of existence, a Kohinoor in the royal crown of life. To carry out any activity, in your life, you use three instruments:

1. Time
2. Energy
3. Mind

1) Time: In any activity of your life, you give your time, you assign your life events to that activity. The importance of an activity spontaneously makes you give more of your time to it. Isn't it?

2) Energy: In any activity, your physical/mental energy, your prana, your life force, is utilized. The value of the activity determines how much energy you need to invest in it. Some activities absorb tremendous amount of energy, while some other activities require only a small amount of life force.

3) Mind: From morning to night, day after day, for any activity, you need to give your attention, your focus to it. Whichever activity you give your mind to, you give your attention to, your whole consciousness, mind, intellect, memory and ego get directed and focused on that particular activity, for that much time. Consider the example of an archer shooting an arrow. The sharp arrowhead is the mind; the stick is intellect and memory combined; and the fin-shaped

fletching, which gives direction to the arrow, is the ego. You, the soul, being the archer, wherever you aim the arrowhead, the whole arrow goes in that direction. Similarly, whichever activity you direct your mind to, give your attention to, your intellect performs all of its five functions in relation to that activity. The memory collects its impressions, tendencies get triggered and the flavours of the ego begin to play their games in that direction.

At this juncture, I want to clarify the meaning of this term 'mind'. As discussed before, there are two prevalent schools of thought. A section of explorers, when they use the word 'mind', include mind, intellect, memory and ego, all these four modes of your individual consciousness, in that term. Whenever the expression 'mind' is used, they mean the whole inner world, the whole arrow. Another school of thought which goes further in this exploration refers to these four sections as separate from each other. Its explorers have very intricately identified and defined the three functions of the mind, the five functions of the intellect, the two sections of memory and a few flavours of the ego. In this topic of the book, when I use the word 'mind', I am including all four modes with their individual functions; I am referring to the whole arrow.

If you minutely observe all around us, every individual soul is giving these three precious instruments—of time-energy-mind—to the activities of their own lives. One more layer of the truth: though these three instruments are distinct and separate from each other, the main player is the mind. Wherever you give your attention, whichever activity you put your mind to, your time and energy get utilized there. Isn't it? My point is, though time and energy are extremely precious instruments of your life, it is the mind that plays the whole game. It is the mind that gives direction to your time and energy as well. It is the mind that attends to the issues of life. Take reference of all the six aspects of your own life: your relationships, profession, hobbies, physical health, social responsibilities and spiritual growth. You will see that whichever aspect you have devoted your attention to, your whole presence, your whole energy gets utilized in that direction and that particular area develops, grows, blossoms in direct proportion to the amount of time and attention you have given it.

By now you would have realized how the individual consciousness is at play in all aspects of your existence. As your consciousness gets more refined, higher stages of evolution open up for you.

II. The three directions you seek happiness from

Let us explore one more layer of the truth. In its pursuit of happiness, of sukh you give your mind in three directions:

1) Seeking validation from wordly achievements.
2) Seeking pleasure from the five senses.
3) Experiencing Ananda through sadhana, satsang, seva.

In the Bhagavad Gita, Bhagavan Shri Krishna says:

यदग्रे चानुबन्धे च सुखं मोहनमात्मनः ।
निद्रालस्यप्रमादोत्थं तत्तामसमुदाहृतम् ।।
(Chapter XVIII: Verse 39)

The illusion of pleasure that arises from unawareness and inadvertence, which at the beginning and also in the end serves to delude the self, is termed as tamasik pleasure, leading to ignorance, dullness and darkness.

विषयेन्द्रियसंयोगाद्यत्तदग्रेऽमृतोपमम् ।
परिणामे विषमिव तत्सुखं राजसं स्मृतम् ।।
(Chapter XVIII: Verse 38)

The pleasure which arises from the union of the senses with sense objects and which in the beginning has a luring, sweet flavour but is like poison in the end is known as rajasik pleasure.

यत्तदग्रे विषमिव परिणामेऽमृतोपमम् ।
तत्सुखं सात्विकं प्रोक्तमात्मबुद्धिप्रसादजम् ॥
(Chapter XVIII: Verse 37)

That joy which demands effort and discipline in the beginning but ensures benevolence and bliss, is like the very nectar of life towards the end and is termed as satvik pleasure.

1) Seeking validation from worldly achievements

This is where the mind seeks joy, fulfilment and satisfaction from achieving material possessions and worldly success. However, as we have discussed in the topic of shadripu, in the section of lobh-moh (greed-attachments), this is merely an illusion. Hence it is called tamasik sukh delusionary pleasure. Look how much of your time-energy-mind is utilized in seeking happiness from this outer world. Until you possessed something, achieved something, till you reached somewhere, the illusion kept on luring you, making you restless, feverish, dependent. But as soon as you arrived, achieved, possessed, inevitably and invariably, every single time, the soap bubble burst, leaving you empty-handed, disillusioned, fooled. This outer world cannot give you anything, because it is not designed to give you anything. Hence it is called Maya, illusion. It has also been given the title of 'mirage', an optical illusion, *mrigjal*.

The mirage analogy will help you understand this phenomenon better. On a hot summer day, in a dry desert-like surrounding, you clearly see a water body on the horizon, but as you walk towards it and reach that spot, there's no water to be found—it always goes further away; it never quenches your thirst. Very similarly, till you achieve these worldly possessions, they give you an illusion of happiness, achievement, success. But as you achieve them, they always leave you empty-handed and thirsty for more. *Neither is Maya designed to give you higher insights, nor is it meant to enhance your energies or offer you any happiness. On the contrary, it is guaranteed to waste your precious time, drain your most valuable energy and is destined to contaminate your pleasant, happy mind.*

I am not saying it is wrong to possess the world. I am not saying you should not work towards achieving material success. In the process of evolution, when the soul is in the body, it is almost obliged to perform the chores, the duties, the formalities of being in this world, society and family. Since we have this body, whether we like it or not, whether we agree with it or not, many of these outer-world activities are almost forced upon us, from jobs to businesses to social responsibilities to maintenance of families and so on. All I am saying is, there is no guarantee of satisfaction, fulfilment and happiness through this accumulation and hoarding of people-things-situations. In short, the ultimate purpose of evolution is lost. The precious opportunity of being in the human body is missed. The full blossoming of an individual consciousness is compromised. *As the soul evolves and as deeper, higher, subtler truths are realized, one understands the futility, the worthlessness, the 'drama', of having to take care of worldly matters. Hence this game of Maya, of the outer world, is branded as tamasik sukh, delusionary pleasure.*

In Bhaja Govindam, Adi Shankara says:

मा कुरु धनजनयौवनगर्व
हरति निमेषात्काल: सर्वम् ।
मायामयमिदमखिलं हित्वा
ब्रह्मपदं त्वं प्रविश विदित्वा ।।

Do not take pride in your wealth, associations and youth. Each one of these perishes within a moment in time. Free yourself from this world of Maya and attain *'Brahmapadam'*, the highest state!

2) Seeking pleasure from the five senses

As established before, our desire for happiness, pleasantness, bliss is the main driving force of your life. Every activity you do to attain that happiness is like a two-sided coin. Some activities give you initial pleasure, initial comfort, but soon the coin flips and the same activity starts reducing your happiness and draining your energy. Contrary to this, some other activities demand your attention, your discipline, your committed effort initially, but eventually yield rich and long-term rewards. In the endeavour of Ananda, many times the mind seeks the five sensory pleasures—of watching, listening, smelling, tasting and touching. However, these sensory pleasures are limited and temporary.

Let us understand this phenomenon through some examples. One of the most alluring sensory pleasures is the pleasure we derive from eating delicious food. Even when you are really hungry, see how quickly you arrive at the limit of this sensory pleasure. The threshold of your capacity to enjoy is achieved in just a few minutes. If you continue to eat for the sake of taste, it makes you feel heavy, dull, groggy and lethargic in a short while. Your level of awareness, energy and pleasantness dramatically drop for the next few hours. Your efficiency, your effectiveness, your interest, your sense of responsibility, your ability to celebrate—all of it takes a big hit. Similarly, if you like a song or a piece of music, how long can you listen to it? Initially you enjoy it, but in a short while the joy diminishes. Some people have the habit of keeping the radio on for hours. In a little while, their mind becomes so desensitized to the sound that they can hardly even hear it. Just the noise remains. Enjoyment or pleasure is a far-fetched idea.

Some people have the habit of putting on a strong perfume, which gives a headache to the people around them, whereas their own nose gets so used to the perfume that they can't smell it anymore. Look what happens when you watch TV or browse social media. The enthusiasm with which you start browsing gradually declines. In a short while, it makes you dull, lazy and heavy.

In the shadripu segment of this book, we have discussed in detail the sensory pleasure of touch and its effects. On the one hand, the sense of touch can invoke a very sweet flavour of connection, belongingness, togetherness among people; on the other hand, excessive touching, cuddling, hugging dramatically drain and disperse your personal energy. Hence in many evolved spiritual traditions it is proclaimed, 'स्पर्शम् पापम्', in reference to the demerits of excessive touching.

Minute observation will reveal that in the domain of sensory pleasures, all the five senses are designed to give you a definite amount of pleasure, with their very shallow limits. The sense of smell can't give you the pleasure or joy equivalent to what the sense of taste can. In the five senses, the capacity of each sensory pleasure is almost predetermined, with the sense of touch (sex, masturbation) offering the highest sensory pleasure. Look at this interesting design of life. Almost directly proportional to the amount of pleasure a particular sense organ can give you, when the coin flips, it also causes an equivalent drop in the amount of energy.

The domain of the worldly pleasures is that of hallucination, illusion, mirage, a fool's paradise . . . the yearning of a *rogi*! In the realm of rajasik sukh, temporary indulgences and attractions culminate into the inevitable drainage of pleasantness, purity and integrity. Hence it is called *vyabhichar*, decadence . . . the act of a *bhogi*.

3) Achieving bliss, Ananda, through sadhana-satsang-seva

We are about to discuss the third category of activities which initially demand skillful, disciplined efforts but eventually lead to extraordinary and long-lasting blossoming of the consciousness. The activities that can dramatically enhance the quality of your life are:

1. Sadhana (individual practice)
2. Satsang (being in association with deeper and higher truths)
3. Seva (service)

III. Sadhana: The transformative practices of yoga, pranayama, Sudarsha Kriya, meditation and chanting

In their exploration of realities, the wise rishis derived specific techniques and processes to refine, polish and upgrade your individual body-mind complex. To keep the body flexible, supple and healthy, they designed different postures of yogasanas. To unfold the secret powers of the breath, they discovered different methods of pranayamas. To utilize the enchanting effects of sounds, they formulated specific mantras and ragas to invoke abundance of all kinds in the collective consciousness. For the optimum utilization of the infinite powers of mind, intellect, memory and ego, they derived *yamas* and *niyamas*, disciplines of individual existence and disciplines of social behaviour. For achieving the highest realization of *Aham Brahmasmi*, universal consciousness, they offered various techniques to attain samadhi, meditation. Regular and committed practise of these life-transforming techniques—of yogasanas, pranayama, Sudarshan Kriya, chanting mantras and meditation—is called sadhana.

Maintaining utmost reverence and respect, when a sincere seeker performs these sacred ceremonies of sadhana, the individual consciousness experiences freedom from deep impressions, release of negative emotions, instantaneous enhancement of energy, profound peace and tranquility at mental and emotional levels. Sadhana empowers your individual consciousness so profoundly that the influence of the outer world (people-situation-things) starts diminishing.

Rather than getting affected by the situations, you start influencing the environment around you. *In a ruffled, restless, scattered mind, cluttered with thoughts, emotions and impressions, deeper realizations cannot happen. Sadhana creates the required stillness, emptiness and focus in your inner world, where subtler insights can occur; it creates a fertile platform for higher truth to dawn.* About Sadhana, the learned ones have proclaimed that it is the *dhan*, the wealth that will be carried forward with the soul, even after the body is dropped. All other types of wealth instantaneously fall away as soon as the breath breaks and the body dies. Just a few minutes of sadhana every day can transform the quality of the rest of the day. Hence it is called satvik sukh, initial committed efforts, resulting in an explosive expansion of the consciousness.

My own life has been tremendously nourished by the techniques of sadhana that I got from the Art of Living courses developed by *pujya* Gurudev. I recommend that you visit the website *artofliving.org*, find an Art of Living centre close to you and experience their curriculum meant for the complete blossoming of the consciousness. It will give you methodical processes to practise every day at home, like Sudarshan Kriya, Sahaj Samadhi (meditation) and many other guided meditation processes designed by pujya Gurudev.

IV. Satsang: Invoking the beautiful amalgamation of devotion and wisdom in your individual consciousness

Satsang has two sections:

- Singing, chanting, celebrating
- Realization and sharing of the truth

1) Singing, chanting, celebrating

In ancient vedic culture the chanting of mantras and the singing of devotional songs in praise of the Divine have always been recommended. The power of the human mind to create its own reality has always been put to work. *When you acknowledge, appreciate and celebrate all the abundance that has been showered on you, your sense of gratitude makes it grow even further. When your focus is on lack, lack grows; when your focus is on abundance, abundance grows.*

Throughout the world, in almost all ancient cultures, the universe, Brahman, the ocean of consciousness, the paramatma was always perceived as the Omnipotent, Omnipresent, Omniscient, Divine, Supernatural entity. And everything in it—from the sun to the moon to the stars to the oceans to the mountains to the rivers to the rains to fire to air—was always seen as portions, sections, chunks of the Divine energy. They were always revered, honoured, worshipped. *The wise seers knew that if humans honour and respect nature, it will always protect them and provide for them. Hence they formulated this ritual, this tradition, this practice of singing praises of the Divine, expressing your thankfulness and requesting-praying-pleading for whatever you want, with a clear belief that 'whatever will be asked for, shall be given'.*

The nature, universe, the Divine, is always poised to proclaim, '*Tathastu*', let thy will be done, so be it ('तुम जो चाहो, सो हो'). Some call it the law of attraction. Whatever you allow to develop in your inner world, you will attract that in the form of things or events in your outer world. *The intensity of your prayer vastly determines how quickly tathastu (so be it) happens.*

The spiritual masters proclaimed:

जो इच्छा करे मन माही, प्रभु प्रताप कछु दुर्लभ नाहिं।

In a pure, pious, uncontaminated mind, whatever wish, desire, intention or prayer arises, the collective consciousness, Brahman, Divinity is poised to fulfil it.

A regular practice to express gratitude for life, to convert your desires and wishes into prayers and to offer them to the Divine—this is the first part of satsang.

2) Realization and sharing of truth

In the second section of satsang, the literal meaning of this word is addressed. *Sat* is truth, knowingness; *sang* is association. Being in association with the ultimate truth is satsang. Even the writing or reading of this book is a part of it. I am honestly expressing the intricate truths that I have explored in my life, and you are courageously, inquisitively and open-heartedly reading them. While reading and contemplating about them, if you instinctively feel that your personal truth is being addressed, that your understanding of the consciousness is getting enriched, that you are finding practical use of this knowledge in dealing with the issues of your life, please be generous, courageous and responsible and share it with others.

In India, where universal consciousness and individual consciousness have been studied for millennia, the rishis have documented their extraordinary findings in the form of a few scriptures. Extremely meticulous, methodical, detailed descriptions of all aspects of the consciousness are available in such holy manuscripts as the Bhagavad Gita, Srimad Bhagavatam, Patanjali Yog Sutras, Narada Bhakti Sutras, Ashtavakra Gita, Yoga Vasistha, etc. From *bhakti* (devotion), gyan (knowledge), *dhyan* (meditation) to *swar* (power of breath) and *mantra* (the magic of chanting)—everything is explored extensively in these scriptures for the benefit of humanity. I recommend that, with utmost reverence and respect, you go through these divine scriptures for the blossoming of your own consciousness. Reading open-heartedly the narrations of truth by the learned ones; regularly reminding yourself of the deeper, higher truths of existence, so that the mind doesn't lose the path of self-realization; and taking reference of the holy scriptures to explore the true nature of the self—all this is part of satsang. In the domain of swadhyay on a very regular basis, observing your tendencies, your conversations and the platform or base on which they sustain is also part of sat-sang, being in association with the deeper truths of life.

V. Seva: Sa–Iva, becoming like the Divine with selfless service

As we approach the finish line, the final chapter, the crescendo, let us look at the whole path of evolution of an individual soul. I want to invite you to visualize it as a pyramid. As one climbs higher and higher on the pyramid, there is lesser and lesser space up there. Similarly, in the journey of evolution, as infinite number of souls ascend one level after another in their maturity and refinement of individual consciousness, there are fewer and fewer souls up there. You can clearly see this phenomenon at work in the world around you. In any field—from business to arts to politics to sports to spirituality—as you go higher, there are fewer and fewer people up there in their respective fields.

In the process of evolution, billions of people, those who have graduated to be in the human form now, are incessantly, compulsively, almost blindly wasting away their precious time, energy and mind, seeking to draw pleasure, comfort and security from the games of the outer world, from people-situations-things, tamasik sukh, delusionary pleasures. Getting almost nothing in return, yet blinded, hypnotized, mesmerized by the play of Maya, they keep believing that the worldly achievements and material possessions will satisfy them, fulfil them, validate their existence. Look at the sheer volume of people playing this blind game of Maya, forming the wide base of the pyramid. Many, many others are seeking pleasures through the five senses, rajasik sukh, getting small amounts of pleasure from smelling, hearing, watching, tasting and touching, where the joy is very limited and short-lived, but there is a massive drop in the levels of awareness, energy and happiness almost instantaneously.

Visualize a soul passing through all the yonis and entering the Homo sapiens–human kingdom, spending dozens of lifetimes, gradually evolving, experiencing extreme dependence on the illusionary games of tamasik sukh, the temporary attractions of rajasik sukh, and taking the first step into the realm of satvik sukh in the form of sadhana. As the evolution continues, an inevitable stage comes where the soul gets instinctively interested in *satya-sang*; it wants to know higher truths, immerses itself in self-exploration, swadhyay. As the soul approaches the extreme top of the pyramid of evolution, the final frontier is that of seva, service, being useful.

Gurudev often says that seva is *Sa Iva*, the process of becoming like Him, the Divine, the Almighty. Nature continuously, incessantly, unconditionally keeps providing *everything for everyone*, without prejudice, bias or expectation of any kind. The sun shines for life to continue, the oceans provide us with clouds that bring us lifesaving rain, the wind supports pollination for the vegetation to foster, fire brings warmth that kindles fertility. *This Omnipotent, Omnipresent, Omniscient, Divine entity called nature, existence, the universe, is in a continuous, unconditional giving mode.* In the final stage of evolution of an individual soul, the training is to become like the Divine. Drop your resistance, release your smallness and with a playful, prayerful, devotional mind, get ready to be useful to the creation, to become the instrument of the Divine—for the betterment of the collective consciousness of your society, of your nation, of the whole world. Courageously take up this higher responsibility and inspire other souls to walk on the path of righteousness, correctness, Dharma.

A simple definition of seva-service is, *'Through your effort of manasa, vacha, karmana (being, speaking, doing), if someone gets to know the higher truths of life, someone's energy levels get enhanced and someone experiences heightened levels of joy— seva is happening. Through your timely intervention, if some soul experiences freedom from the clutches of Maya, the illusion or the luring of the five sensory pleasures, and gets committed towards sadhana, satsang, seva—seva is happening. If you become the instrument for someone's consciousness, to take that step forward towards higher evolution—seva is happening.'*

In short, if your life is an example where people recognize the futility of tamasik and rajasik pleasures, and if your words and actions exhibit the infinite strength of satvik sukh, seva is happening.

In the domain of seva, let us be clear about these few obstacles. In spite of knowing the transformative effect of this highest-value activity of human existence, seva—beware of the play of ego, the inferiority complex, the smallness. There are a few traits of this ego which do not allow you to take this plunge. For example, sometimes a lack of self-confidence prevents you from taking up higher responsibilities. Sometimes it's the fear of failure that becomes a hindrance.

Sometimes, in spite of knowing everything, sheer lethargy, laziness, *pramad* takes over and you are simply unable to jump into action.

Let us now revisit this whole exploration from the perspective of your own individual evolution. No matter how much *time, energy* and *mind* you give to the outer world of Maya, satisfaction, contentment and fulfilment doesn't happen. You can gather people around you, accumulate things for yourself and create desired situations, but the *ultimate blossoming* eludes you. Rajasik sukh can add a little bit of interest in your life, through beautiful colours, melodious music, delicious tastes, etc. But it eventually creates bondage and dependence. It attaches your mind to sensory pleasures, offering very little and very temporary sukh while draining your most precious life force, the prana. It contaminates your naturally beautiful, potent mind and distracts the direction of your life, away from the ultimate blossoming.

As you dive deep into your personal sadhana, you experience a tremendous blast of kundalini shakti, the life force. Your mind settles down, paving the way for deeper, higher truths to dawn. Through satsang, on the one hand, you gratefully celebrate all the gifts from the Divine; on the other hand, you explore the potentialities of the macrocosm and the microcosm, of the ocean and the wave, of paramatma and jivatma, existence and you. The optimum culmination is in seva. All that empowering energy, thankfulness for having received treasures from life and meticulous understanding of your existence and your own role in it has to ultimately result in you, the individual soul, becoming the instrument for the blossoming of other souls. In short, *'Seva is wisdom in action.'*

As you take higher responsibility, your area of influence grows and you get the opportunity of expanding the arena of your existence. *Higher seva exposes your strengths as well as your weaknesses. But look at this benevolent design of the consciousness. When your strengths, your positives, your pluses, get exposed, they always grow, expand, get strengthened. And when your weaknesses, your shortcomings, your limitations get exposed, they always break, dissolve, free you and go away. It is the higher responsibility of seva that gives you this unique, powerful, transformational opportunity of exposing and growing your strengths, as well as of exposing and breaking your limitations.*

I recommend, take up the seva of enrolling people in practising Sudarshan Kriya and meditation every day. Take up the seva of inspiring others for swadhyay, self-exploration. Take up the seva of orienting people in Brahma Gyan, the knowledge of existence. If this book has helped you in your personal journey, take up the seva of gifting it to your near and dear ones.

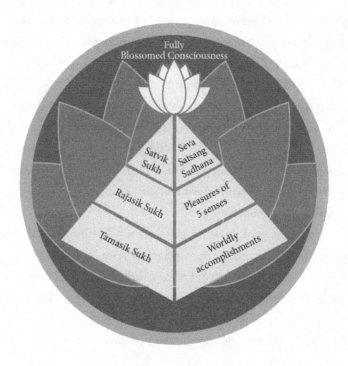

The Pyramid of Evolution

Worksheet

Make a note of all the 'pearls of wisdom' that you would like to retain from this chapter for your future reference

....

....

....

....

....

....

....

....

....

....

....

....

....

....

....

....

....

....

....

....

....

....

....

Have a general overview of your own life and make a note of how much of your time, energy and mind is being given in which direction and what you are getting in return

Tamasik Sukh: Seeking validation from vyakti, vastu, paristhiti, the outer world

....
....
....
....
....
....
....
....

Rajasik Sukh: Seeking five sensory pleasures

....
....
....
....
....
....
....
....

Satvik Sukh: Experiencing the blossoming of consciousness through sadhana-satsang-seva

....
....
....
....
....
....
....
....
....
....
....
....
....
....
....
....
....
....
....
....
....
....
....
....
....
....
....
....

Your commitment to sadhana-satsang-seva
Sadhana: Learn and commit yourself to the daily practice of yogasan, pranayama, Sudarshan Kriya and meditation

....

....

....

....

....

....

....

....

....

Satsang: Commit yourself to daily chanting, daily reading of scriptures and contemplation of knowledge

....

....

....

....

....

....

....

....

....

....

Seva: Commit yourself to be an instrument of transformation for as many people as you can and design your seva here

....

....

....

....

....

....

....

....

....

....

....

....

....

Step Six

Designing Your Life

Time to consolidate all the knowledge into personal commitments, to give the desired direction to your life. Having explored the intricacies of the consciousness, having identified the six enemies, having learnt the techniques of becoming free from them, having realized the futility of the outer-world activities, having recognized the extreme limitedness of the sensory pleasures, having understood the importance of sadhana, satsang and seva, we are now ready for this final step. It is time for *sankalpas*, commitments. It is the time to design how you want to live your life.

I. Personal commitments to a celebratory life

I want to offer some potent guidelines, in the form of a few aphorisms, sutras, that can help you maintain your march on the right track, save your mind from reverse gears and ensure uninterrupted progress towards the full blossoming.

1. Take responsibility for your unconditional happiness, pleasantness and purity

In spite of the ups and downs of this rollercoaster ride of life, profits or losses, favourable or non-favourable situations, commit yourself to maintaining pleasantness, positiveness and purity in your inner world. For that, use your ability to let go of the negatives and keep invoking enthusiasm, love and celebration. Learn to separate the games of the outer world and the flavours of the inner world. You may not have too much control over situations and circumstances, but a trained, skilful, determined mind always has the choice to drop unpleasantness, impurity, and to maintain unconditional happiness, pleasantness and purity within.

2. Take responsibility for others' blossoming

Wherever you go, whoever you meet, see if you can be the instrument for their journey from negative to neutral, or from neutral to positive. Take responsibility for the blossoming of their consciousness by inspiring them towards transformative ways of sadhana, satsang and seva. As soon as you willingly pick up this responsibility, your infinitely powerful intellect will find its own ways to make it happen. Learn to sensitively observe the condition people are in and sense the state of their mind. Experiment with and learn from the opportunities that life offers you to contribute in people's lives. Sensitively make them aware about the shadripus and their harmful influences. Skilfully bring people into an *open-hearted listening mode*. When they are willing to learn, teach them how easy it is to drop the negatives and to invoke the positives.

If this book has contributed to your life, you may want to gift a few copies of it to your near and dear ones. Once your ecosystem, your family members, your friends and colleagues are oriented in this transformative way of swadhyay, dealing with challenges and handling issues of life with them becomes much more effortless for you. You can start with your first orbit, with the people who are closest to you, and gradually expand your horizons. Once you take up this higher responsibility of bringing people on the right path, you will notice how effortlessly your own consciousness maintains its positive, pleasant and pure state. *The more you become an instrument in the process of someone's learning, the more you teach, the more you learn.*

3. Identify the flavours that inspire you and commit yourself to invoking them regularly

I want to share something that is very close to my heart: a personal, intimate, sacred truth of my life. Since the early days of my spiritual journey, with the extremely valuable guidance of my mentor, my teacher, my guide, my Gurudev, I got the opportunity of exploring the personal and universal consciousness to its minutest detail. After years of this expedition, I came to the conclusion that I have the freedom and responsibility to choose the flavours of consciousness that call me, inspire me and fulfil me.

Among the range of flavours that can be derived from the *bhakti rasa* (devotion), *vairagya rasa* (dispassion), *veer rasa* (valour), *karuna rasa* (compassion), etc., these four flavours inspire me the most: Truth, Love, Responsibility and Celebration.

- Through my satsangs and devotional rock concerts, almost every day of my life, I invoke intense, exhilarating, mind-blowing celebrations.
- Through my intensely honest knowledge sessions, I invoke the deepest and highest truths that help millions to explore their true nature. My observation: As soon as the truth is addressed, it sets you free.
- I feel responsibility is the most transformative flavour. In any field of your life, the amount of responsibility you take gives you equivalent opportunity to play, to participate and to contribute. Responsibility is like the area of your influence. Whichever aspects of your life you have taken responsibility in, you live, you exist, you thrive in those areas. It is the responsibility that gives you the power, the inner strength to make things better. *It is the responsibility that gives you the opportunity to own whatever is happening, whatever is missing and whatever is possible in any area of your life. The inherent difference between duty and responsibility is that duty is imposed upon you, whereas responsibility is always taken willingly.*

Responsibility is your ability to respond to the need of the moment. It is almost like a rule, a principle, a law according to which the human consciousness functions. *Responsibility increases power.*

An interesting turth: *your emotions, your choices, your actions, your decisions, your happiness, your Dharma, the blossoming of your consciousness, all of it is your own responsibility. In short, your life is your responsibility.* Whichever area of your life you want to strengthen, take complete responsibility for it and committedly go behind it. Let your inner powers, your siddhis blossom fully. *I have always seen my Gurudev taking responsibility for the whole world, and I have directly learnt that from him. Responsibility inspires me, expands my being, brings me closer to the Divine.*

- Love is the driving force of my life. Love makes me soft, love makes me humble, love dissolves me. Wherever love is invoked, almost spontaneously, responsibility is taken. I feel that love and responsibility are almost synonyms, they go hand in hand. *Love invokes ownership, and ownership generates responsibility.* I love this existence and everything in it, and I feel responsible for the whole creation.

In whichever relationship love, belongingness, oneness and ownership are triggered in my life, naturally and effortlessly, complete responsibility for the blossoming of that soul is instinctively taken. Truth is the instrument of that transformation. These four flavours—Celebration, Truth, Responsibility and Love—are the driving forces of my life.

I invite you to identify and shortlist the flavours of the consciousness that motivate, inspire and energize you. Commit yourself to invoking them regularly for a substantial amount of time, till their habits or tendencies get intensified in your mind and it becomes easier for you to invoke any flavour at will, on demand, whenever and wherever you want. So my point is, let us optimally utilize this unique opportunity of being in the human body to create the mind, the inner world, the way you want it. Let us use the events, situations, circumstances of this lifetime as a practice ground. When we take higher responsibility, a wide range of situations and circumstances get created, where your commitment of holding on to these benevolent flavours is challenged. In spite of these challenges, when you train your mind with 'committed skilful efforts', it gets oriented into maintaining the beauty within. As in video games, once you learn to play the higher, more difficult, more challenging levels, playing the lower, easier levels becomes effortless.

4. Upholding Dharma

Finally it will boil down to this defining step. Time to understand the illusionary games of Maya and the infinitely benevolent practice of Dharma. As established before, the illusionary accolades of worldly achievements and the temporary, short-lived pleasures of the five senses are the play of Maya, where ultimately the soul experiences wastage of time, extreme energy drops, contamination and bondage of the mind. Whereas these two transformative steps that ensure the full blossoming of the soul are the domain of Dharma:

1. Using the three transformative instruments of your attention, the outgoing breath and your ability to surrender, being free from the harmful tendencies of the shadripus.
2. Exploring the infinite possibilities of sadhana, satsang and seva, where there is no limit to how much you can expand your individual consciousness and become one with the Divine.

I want to invite you for a paradigm shift at this juncture. This marvellous opportunity of being in the human form can be lived with these two extreme perspectives. First, where you feel you are a soul living in Maya, obliged, forced, compelled to take care of *vyavhar vyavasay*, the worldly formalities of profession, families and society. Fatigued, disillusioned, tired, you periodically come to the transformative domain of Dharma and recharge your batteries through sadhana, satsang, seva, but ultimately have to helplessly go back to your worldly chores.

There is an extremely beautiful way of life available—where you declare yourself to be a representative of Dharma, you believe sadhana-satsang-seva is the way and attaining Salvation, Liberation, Nirvana is your goal. While you are using this life to attain 'Project Moksha', skilfully and playfully you take care of the worldly activities of Maya as well, unabetted, untouched and unruffled.

I joyfully invite you, humbly request you and intensely urge you to take this courageous leap of faith and declare yourself to be the holder of Dharma. With sensitive care, withdraw your mind gradually from the clutches of Maya, commit yourself to the regular practice of sadhana, satsang and seva, and optimally use your instruments of Time, Energy and Mind to attain the highest *param tatva. As you bring about this paradigm shift to uphold Dharma, you will see a miracle unfolding. The Divine presence will regularly bless you: 'Tathastu . . . So be it.' Mysteriously, magically, almost miraculously, you keep manifesting your own reality, of the highest truth, vibrant aliveness and intense bliss!*

II. The Guru, the Path: Importance of a mentor, a guide, a personal navigator

On this abstract path of exploring the self and the Divine, throughout centuries, the learned ones, the rishis, the seers have emphasized on the value of having a Guru, a mentor, a teacher.

The wise ones have proclaimed:

गुरु कुंभार शिष कुंभ है, गढ़ि गढ़ि काढ़ै खोट
अन्तर हाथ सहार दै, बाहर बाहै चोट।

The Guru, the master, is like an extremely skilled potter, who gives shape to soft clay and makes it into a beautiful pot. As the raw, unprepared pot takes shape, he protects it from the inside and gives it the cushioning of his palm, while from outside he firmly taps and thuds.

गुरु गोविन्द दोऊ खड़े, काके लागुं पाय,
बलिहारी गुरु आपने, गोविन्द दियो बताय।

I see the Guru and the God standing side by side. Whom should I first bow down to? My devoted mind says, let me prostrate myself at the lotus feet of my Gurudev, who introduced me to the Divine.

The learned ones have visualized this path of spiritual blossoming as a staircase made up of soap. Now imagine that it's also raining heavily while the seeker is climbing up this slippery soap ladder. The Guru, the teacher, is like the balustrade, the railing. If you do not have that support to cling on to, it's almost impossible for you to make it to the top of this abstract, slippery slope.

The seeker of truth, the explorer of Brahman, would definitely require the guidance of someone who has travelled on this adventurous path before, someone who knows the intricacies of the journey, someone who has successfully overcome the challenges and has figured out a way to *make it to the top of the pyramid*. The Guru is someone who understands your individual stage of evolution; someone who instinctively knows the step forward for you; someone who also understands your strengths and weaknesses; and someone who would sensitively, delicately, yet firmly hold your hand to guide you to walk this transformative path of Dharma, one step after the other.

For me, my Gurudev is my Krishna, my Shiva, my Divine. He is like the air I breathe. His invisible, unseen presence, is the guiding force of my life. Whatever I am today is all because of his precious guidance and his infinite grace. Throughout these two and a half decades, I have had the opportunity of travelling with my Gurudev to many countries. I am flabbergasted at the effect he has on the people and on the environment around Him. From flamboyant Americans to devotional Indians to very stern and sincere Germans, from heads of states and extremely wealthy businessmen to young, open-hearted students—everyone around Him is thoroughly soaked in his energy of intense love, deep silence and sheer compassion. People's hearts blossom, happy devotional tears flow and an inexplicable bliss dawns in His divine presence. Everywhere he goes, in His silence people find the answers to their questions. In His words, millions attain guidance for their own blossoming. When He meditates, the whole existence quietens down and becomes still. When He takes up mammoth service projects, the whole universe conspires to make them a reality. With His wisdom and uncanny perspective, He resolves the most complicated conflicts among people, among religions, among nations. The path of the Art of Living that he has created is a miracle in itself. All the ingredients one requires for one's own *complete blossoming* are interwoven so beautifully on this path. *From extremely deep meditations to mind-blowing celebrations, from the highest knowledge of existence to heart-wrenching devotion and life-transforming service, everything that one requires for the complete blossoming of their individual consciousness is put together in such an effortless amalgamation on this path.*

Almost 5000 years ago, Lord Krishna gave the transformative scripture of the Bhagavad Gita to the world, in which he spoke of attaining the highest form of wisdom, Brahma Gyan, through Dhyan Yoga, Gyan Yoga, Bhakti Yoga and Karma Yoga. My Gurudev has repackaged the same Brahma Gyan, the knowledge of existence, to suit the contemporary times and has given us sadhana, satsang, seva.

In sadhana, through yogasanas, pranayama, Sudarshan Kriya and extremely powerful guided meditations, he effortlessly takes us to *turiya awastha*, the transcendental stage, the *samadhi stithi*. This is nothing but Dhyan Yoga.

Through satsang, he gives us extremely simplified sutras of the Art of Living, the knowledge of Brahman, in such a way that even young, raw, untrained minds can understand it—which is the essence of Gyan Yoga. One extraordinary thing happens in His discourses: even though lakhs of people are listening to Him at a time, each one experiences a personal connection with Him, as if He is directly talking to them, guiding them about their individual issues. Through songs and celebrations in satsang, he has rekindled the ancient tradition of appreciating, praising and adoring the Divine, which is Bhakti Yoga. Satsang is a combination of Gyan Yoga and Bhakti Yoga.

Through seva, He has given to millions around the world the opportunity of becoming instruments of transformation. So far, He has made more than 25,000 teachers of Art of Living courses across 156 countries and has trained over 2,00,000 *yuvacharyas*, youth leaders, from rural India who are oriented extensively in seva. *Rather than focusing on 'what will I get, what is in it for me', Gurudev has invoked this beautiful essence of seva, of 'how can I help', 'how can I be useful', 'how can I selflessly serve', in millions of minds.* This willingness to be the instrument of transformation is the very essence of Karma Yoga.

About 2500 years ago, when the Buddha attained enlightenment, it is believed that his presence guided 10,000 people to experience nirvana. Through the gift of sadhana-satsang-seva that my Gurudev has given to the world, millions of souls have awakened to the joy of their being and are walking on the path to attain Liberation, Salvation, Moksha!

Worksheet

Make a note of all the 'pearls of wisdom' that you would like to retain from this chapter for your future reference

....

....

....

....

....

....

....

....

....

....

....

....

....

....

....

....

....

....

....

....

....

....

....

Enlist what you have learnt through this book

....
....
....
....
....
....
....
....
....
....

*Make a list of the beautiful flavours that inspire you and commit
yourself to invoking them regularly*

....
....
....
....
....
....
....
....
....
....

Make a plan to live a life of 'Dharma' over a life of 'Maya'

....
....
....
....
....
....
....
....
....
....
....
....
....
....
....
....
....
....
....
....
....
....
....
....
....
....
....
....

The Way Forward . . .

Having created the worksheets; having made the lists of tendencies, conversations, platforms that you need to be free from; having committed yourself to the letting go of the shadripus; having made up your mind to regularly practise sadhana, satsang and seva; and having taken the commitment of living the life of Dharma, you are now ready for the way forward!

The individual consciousness intrinsically has all the necessary abilities, powers, siddhis for creating anything and everything that it wants. In the divine scripture of Yoga Vasistha, the learned seer Rishi Vasistha proclaims:

'सब कुछ, सदा ही, सबको उपलब्ध है अगर बीच में प्रयत्न को छोड़ ना दिया जाए तो।'

Everything, all the time, is available to everyone, if committed skilful efforts are not dropped in between.

I wish you a celebratory life! May the Divine become your guiding force!

Practical Applications of Transformative Formulas from *Celebrating Life*: A Six-Session, Life-Changing Video Tutorial Series

Subjects of tutorials

1. Secret of a happy, fulfilling and celebratory life.
2. Importance of taking the right decisions.
3. Identifying all the harmful tendencies and their damaging influence on your life.
4. Practical techniques to be free from all the negativities of life.
5. Swadhyay . . . Recognizing your infinite potential within.
6. Formulas to design your life the way you want it!

If you have bought the tutorial package along with the copy of this book, please check your registered email id for access.

For those who haven't yet registered for the tutorials, please visit www.celebratinglifebook.com.

Hope the reading experience of *Celebrating Life* was uplifting and transformative!

If you wish to experience the complete spiritual syllabus of exploring your own divinity within and would like to take invaluable personal guidance from Rishiji, please send a WhatsApp message on +91 9978666699 or +91 9904661166. Our team will connect with you.

Follow Rishi Nityapragya on social media

Instagram: https://instagram.com/rishinityapragya
YouTube: https://www.youtube.com/rishinityapragya
Facebook: https://www.facebook.com/RishiNityapragya
Twitter: https://twitter.com/Rishiji
LinkedIn: https://www.linkedin.com/in/rishi-nityapragya-63b208143
Website: http://www.rishinityapragya.com/

The *Celebrating Life* app is now available on the App Store and Google Play Store.

The Founder: Gurudev Sri Sri Ravi Shankar

Gurudev Sri Sri Ravi Shankar is a universally revered spiritual and humanitarian leader. His vision of a violence-free, stress-free society through the reawakening of human values has inspired millions to broaden their spheres of responsibility and work towards the betterment of the world. Born in 1956 in southern India, Gurudev was often found deep in meditation as a child. At the age of four, he astonished his teachers by reciting the Bhagavad Gita. He has always had the unique gift of presenting the deepest truths in the simplest of words.

In 1981, Gurudev established the Art of Living Foundation, an educational and humanitarian non-governmental organization that works in special consultative status with the United Nations Economic and Social Council (ECOSOC). Present in over 156 countries, it formulates and implements lasting solutions to conflicts and issues faced by individuals, communities and nations.

In 1997, he founded the International Association for Human Values (IAHV) to foster human values and lead sustainable development projects. Gurudev has reached out to more than 300 million people worldwide through personal interactions, public events, teachings, the Art of Living workshops and humanitarian initiatives. He has brought to the masses ancient practices that were traditionally kept exclusive and has designed many self-development techniques which can easily be integrated into daily life to calm the mind and instil confidence and enthusiasm. One of Gurudev's most unique offerings to the world is the Sudarshan Kriya, a powerful breathing technique that facilitates physical, mental, emotional and social well-being.

Numerous awards have been bestowed upon Gurudev Sri Sri Ravi Shankar, including the Padma Vibhushan (India's second-highest civilian award) and the highest civilian awards from Paraguay, Mongolia and Colombia. Gurudev has addressed several international forums, including the United Nations Millennium World Peace Summit (2000); World Economic Forum (2001, 2003); the World Summit on Ethics and Leadership in Sports at the FIFA headquarters in Zurich (2014, 2016); UNESCO (2015); and parliaments of France, Britain and Norway (2016) among others.

Gurudev has played a key role in conflict resolution across the world, including in Colombia, Kashmir, Iraq, Ivory Coast and the Naxal-inhabited regions of India, among many other places.

The Art of Living: In Service around the World

Founded in 1981 by Gurudev Sri Sri Ravi Shankar, the Art of Living Foundation is engaged in stress-elimination programmes and service initiatives. The organization operates globally in 156 countries with one of the largest volunteer bases in the world and has touched the lives of over 370 million people.

The organization works in special consultative status with the United Nations Economic and Social Council (ECOSOC), participating in a variety of committees and activities related to health and conflict resolution.

In 1997, Gurudev Sri Sri Ravi Shankar also founded the International Association for Human Values (IAHV) to coordinate sustainable development projects, nurture human values and coordinate conflict resolution in association with the Art of Living. In India, Africa and South America, volunteers of two sister organizations of the Art of Living are spearheading sustainable growth in rural communities and have already reached out to 40,212 villages.

The Art of Living movement has spread peace and transformation across communities through diverse humanitarian projects.

For more information, visit www.artofliving.org.